Comptroller's Handbook   CC-EFTA

Consumer Compliance (CC)

Electronic Fund Transfer Act

October 2011

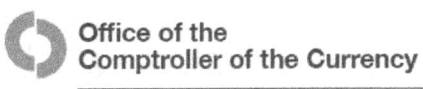

Office of the Comptroller of the Currency

Washington, DC 20219

Electronic Fund Transfer Act— Regulation E

Contents

Electronic Fund Transfer Act— Regulation E

This booklet provides background information and optional expanded examination procedures for the consumer protection regulation on electronic fund transfers (EFT), that is, Regulation E: Electronic Fund Transfers (12 CFR 205).

Because this booklet synopsizes Regulation E, users of this booklet should refer to the regulation for detailed guidance and specific requirements.

After completing a compliance risk assessment, bank examiners should review the applicable examination procedures. For guidance in completing a core assessment, refer to the "Community Bank Supervision," "Large Bank Supervision," and "Internal and External Audits" booklets in the *Comptroller's Handbook*. Complaint information received by the Customer Assistance Group in the Office of the Ombudsman may also be useful in completing the assessment.

Background and Summary

The Electronic Fund Transfer Act (EFTA) (15 USC 1693 et seq.) of 1978 is intended to protect individual consumers engaging in EFTs, which include

- transfers through automated teller machines (ATM),
- point-of-sale (POS) terminals,
- automated clearinghouse (ACH) systems,
- telephone bill-payment plans in which periodic or recurring transfers are contemplated, and
- remote banking programs.

The Board of Governors of the Federal Reserve (Board) implements EFTA through Regulation E, which includes an official staff commentary.

The Board amended Regulation E to add section 205.17, prohibiting institutions from charging overdraft fees for ATM and POS transactions unless the consumer affirmatively consents (74 Fed. Reg. 59033, November 17, 2009; and 75 Fed. Reg. 31665, June 4, 2010). The Board also added section 205.20 to restrict fees and expiration dates on gift cards and to require that gift card terms be clearly stated (75 Fed. Reg. 16580, April 1, 2010).

To help clarify Regulation E requirements mentioned in this booklet, the following background information does not strictly follow the order of the regulatory text. This booklet is arranged in the following order:

I. Scope (Sections 205.2, 205.3, 205.17, 205.20)
II. Disclosures (Sections 205.4, 205.7, 205.8, 205.16, 205.17, 205.20)
III. Electronic Transaction Overdraft Service Opt In (Section 205.17)
IV. Issuance of Access Devices (Sections 205.5, 205.18)
V. Consumer Liability and Error Resolution (Sections 205.6, 205.11)
VI. Receipts and Periodic Statements (Sections 205.9, 205.18)
VII. Gift Cards (Section 205.20)
VIII. Other Requirements (Sections 205.10, 205.14, 205.15)
IX. Relation to Other Laws (Section 205.12)
X. Administrative Enforcement and Record Retention (Section 205.13)
XI. Miscellaneous (EFTA Provisions Not Reflected in Regulation E)

For the examiner's ease of use, the EFTA Worksheet follows the order of the regulation.

I. Scope

Key Definitions

Access device is a card, code, or other means of access to a consumer's account or a combination of these used by the consumer to initiate EFTs. Access devices include debit cards, personal identification numbers (PIN), telephone transfer and telephone bill payment codes, and other means to initiate EFTs to or from a consumer account (section 205.2(a)(1) and staff commentary 205.2(a)–1).

Access devices do not include either of the following:

- Magnetic tape or other devices used internally by a financial institution to initiate EFTs.
- A check or draft used to capture the magnetic ink character recognition (MICR) encoding or routing, account, and serial numbers to initiate a one-time ACH debit (staff commentary 205.2(a)–1 and –2).

Accepted access device is an access device that a consumer

- requests and receives, signs, or uses (or authorizes another to use) to transfer money between accounts or to obtain money, property, or services.
- requests to be validated even if it was issued on an unsolicited basis.
- receives as a renewal or substitute for an accepted access device from either the financial institution that initially issued the device or a successor (section 205.2(a)(2)).

Account includes the following:

- Checking, savings, or other consumer asset account held by a financial institution (directly or indirectly), including certain club accounts, established primarily for personal, family, or household purposes.
- Payroll card account, established through an employer (directly or indirectly), to which EFTs of the consumer's wages, salary, or other employee compensation (such as commissions), are made on a recurring basis. The payroll card account can be operated or managed by the employer, a third-party processor, a depository institution, or any other person. All transactions involving the transfer of funds to or from a payroll card account are covered by the regulation (section 205.2(b)(2) and staff commentary 205.2(b)–2).

An account does not include

- an account held by a financial institution under a bona fide trust agreement.
- an occasional or incidental credit balance in a credit plan.
- profit-sharing and pension accounts established under a bona fide trust agreement.
- escrow accounts, such as for payments of real estate taxes, insurance premiums, or completion of repairs.
- accounts for purchasing U.S. savings bonds (section 205.2(b)(3) and staff commentary 205.2(b)–3).

<u>A payroll card account does not include a card used</u>

- solely to disburse incentive-based payments (other than commissions representing the primary means through which a consumer is paid) that are unlikely to be a consumer's primary source of salary or other compensation.
- solely to make disbursements unrelated to compensation, such as petty cash reimbursements or travel per diem payments.
- in isolated instances, such as when an employer does not make recurring payments (staff commentary 205.2(b)–2).

Activity means any action that results in an increase or decrease of funds underlying a certificate or card, other than the imposition of a fee or an adjustment due to an error or a reversal of a prior transaction (section 205.20(a)(7)).

ATM operator is any person who operates an ATM at which a consumer initiates an EFT or a balance inquiry and who does not hold the account to or from where the transfer is made or about which the inquiry is made (section 205.16(a)).

Dormancy fee and inactivity fee are fees for non-use of or inactivity on a gift certificate, store gift card, or general-use prepaid card (section 205.20(a)(5)).

Electronic check conversion (ECK) transactions are transactions in which a check, draft, or similar paper instrument is used as a source of information to initiate a one-time EFT from a consumer's account. The consumer must authorize the transfer (section 205.3(b)(2)).

Electronic fund transfer is a transfer of funds initiated through an electronic terminal, telephone, computer (including online banking) or magnetic tape for the purpose of ordering, instructing, or authorizing a financial institution to debit or credit a consumer's account. EFTs include, but are not limited to, POS transfers, ATM transfers, direct deposits or withdrawals of funds, transfers initiated by telephone, and transfers resulting from debit card transactions, whether or not initiated through an electronic terminal (section 205.3(b)).

Electronic terminal is an electronic device, other than a telephone call by a consumer, through which a consumer may initiate an EFT. The term includes, but is not limited to, POS terminals, ATMs, and cash-dispensing machines (section 205.2(h)).

Exclusions from gift card definition include the following cards, codes, or other devices, which are not subject to the substantive restrictions on imposing dormancy, inactivity, or service fees or the restrictions on expiration dates, if they are (section 205.20(b))

- usable solely for telephone services.
- reloadable and not marketed or labeled as a gift card or gift certificate. For purposes of this exception, the term "reloadable" includes a temporary non-reloadable card issued solely in connection with a reloadable card, code, or other device.
- a loyalty, award, or promotional gift card (except that these must disclose on the card or device itself such information as the date the funds expire, fee information, and a toll-free number) (sections 205.20(a)(4) and (c)(4)).
- not marketed to the general public.
- issued in paper form only.
- redeemable solely for admission to events or venues at a particular location or group of affiliated locations or to obtain goods or services in conjunction with admission to such events or venues, at the event or venue or at specific locations affiliated with and in geographic proximity to the event or venue.

General-use prepaid card is a card, code, or other device

- issued on a prepaid basis primarily for personal, family, or household purposes to a consumer in a specified amount, whether or not that amount may be increased or reloaded, in exchange for payment.
- that is redeemable upon presentation at multiple, unaffiliated merchants for goods or services or that may be usable at ATMs (section 205.20(a)(3)). *See "Exclusions from gift card definition."*

Gift certificate is a card, code, or other device issued on a prepaid basis primarily for personal, family, or household purposes to a consumer in a specified amount that may not be increased or reloaded in exchange for payment and redeemable upon presentation at a single merchant or an affiliated group of merchants for goods or services (section 205.20(a)(1)). *See "Exclusions from gift card definition."*

Loyalty, award, or promotional gift card is a card, code, or other device

- issued on a prepaid basis primarily for personal, family, or household purposes to a consumer in connection with a loyalty, award, or promotional program.
- that is redeemable upon presentation at one or more merchants for goods or services or usable at ATMs.
- that sets forth certain disclosures, including a statement indicating that the card, code, or other device is issued for loyalty, award, or promotional purposes (section 205.20(a)(4)). *See "Exclusions from gift card definition."*

Overdraft services. A financial institution provides an overdraft service if it assesses a fee or charge for paying a transaction (including a check or other item) when the consumer has insufficient or unavailable funds in the account to pay the transaction. An overdraft service does not, however, include payments made from the following:

- A line of credit subject to Regulation Z, such as a credit card account, a home equity line of credit, or an overdraft line of credit.
- Funds transferred from another account held individually or jointly by the consumer.
- A line of credit or other transaction from a securities or commodities account held by a broker–dealer registered with the U.S. Securities and Exchange Commission (SEC) or the U.S. Commodity Futures Trading Commission (CFTC) (section 205.17(a)).

Preauthorized electronic fund transfer is an EFT authorized in advance to recur at substantially regular intervals (section 205.2(k)).

Service fee is a periodic fee for holding or using a gift certificate, store gift card, or general-use prepaid card. A periodic fee includes any fee that may be imposed on a gift certificate, store gift card, or general-use prepaid card from time to time for holding or using the certificate or card (section 205.20(a)(6)). For example, a service fee may include a monthly maintenance fee, transaction fee, ATM fee, reload fee, foreign currency transaction fee, or balance inquiry fee, whether or not the fee is waived for a certain period of time or is only imposed after a certain period of time. A service fee does not include a one-time fee or a fee that is unlikely to be imposed more than once while the underlying funds are still valid, such as an initial issuance fee, a cash-out fee, a supplemental card fee, or a lost or stolen certificate or card replacement fee (staff commentary 20(a)(6)-1).

Store gift card is a card, code, or other device issued on a prepaid basis primarily for personal, family, or household purposes to a consumer in a specified amount, whether or not that amount may be increased or reloaded, in exchange for payment, and redeemable upon presentation at a single merchant or an affiliated group of merchants for goods or services (section 205.20(a)(2)). *See "Exclusions from gift card definition."*

Unauthorized EFT is an EFT from a consumer's account initiated by a person other than the consumer without authority to initiate the transfer and from which the consumer receives no benefit. This does not include an EFT initiated in any of the following ways:

- By a person who was furnished the access device to the consumer's account by the consumer, unless the consumer has notified the financial institution that transfers by that person are no longer authorized;
- With fraudulent intent by the consumer or any person acting in concert with the consumer; or
- By the financial institution or its employee (section 205.2(m)).

Coverage–Section 205.3

The requirements of Regulation E apply only to accounts for which there is an agreement for EFT services to or from the account between (1) the consumer and the financial institution or (2) the consumer and a third party, when the account-holding financial institution has received notice of the agreement and the fund transfers have begun (staff commentary 205.3(a)–1).

Regulation E applies to all persons, including offices of foreign financial institutions in the United States, that offer EFT services to residents of any state[1] and it covers any account located in the United States through which EFTs are offered to a resident of a state, no matter where a particular transfer occurs or where the financial institution is chartered (staff commentary 205.3(a)–3). Regulation E does not apply to a foreign branch of a U.S. financial institution unless the EFT services are offered in connection with an account in a state, as defined in section 205.2(l) (staff commentary 205.3(a)-3).

---

[1] "State" means any state, territory, or possession of the United States; the District of Columbia; the Commonwealth of Puerto Rico; or any of their political subdivisions (12 CFR 205.2(l)).

Exclusions from coverage: Section 205.3(c) describes transfers that are not EFTs and are therefore not covered by the EFTA and Regulation E:

- Transfers of funds originated by check, draft, or similar paper instrument.
- Check guarantee or authorization services that do not directly result in a debit or credit to a consumer's account.
- Any transfer of funds for a consumer within a system that is used primarily to transfer funds between financial institutions or businesses, e.g., Fedwire or other similar network.
- Any transfer of funds that has as its primary purpose the purchase or sale of securities or commodities regulated by the SEC or the CFTC, purchased or sold through a broker-dealer regulated by the SEC or through a futures commission merchant regulated by the CFTC, or held in book-entry form by a Federal Reserve Bank or federal agency.
- Intra-institutional automatic transfers under an agreement between a consumer and a financial institution.
- Transfers initiated by telephone between a consumer and a financial institution, provided the transfer is not a function of a written plan contemplating periodic or recurring transfers. A written statement available to the public, such as a brochure, that describes a service allowing a consumer to initiate transfers by telephone constitutes a written plan.
- Preauthorized transfers to or from accounts at financial institutions with assets of less than $100 million on the preceding December 31. Such preauthorized transfers, however, remain subject to the compulsory use prohibition under section 913 of the EFTA and 12 CFR 205.10(e), as well as the civil and criminal liability provisions of sections 915 and 916 of the EFTA. A small financial institution that provides EFT services besides preauthorized transfers must comply with the Regulation E requirements for those other services (staff commentary 205.3(c)(7)–1). For example, a small financial institution that offers ATM services must comply with Regulation E concerning the issuance of debit cards, terminal receipts, periodic statements, and other requirements.

Electronic Check Conversion and Collection of Returned-Item Fees

Regulation E covers ECK transactions. In an ECK transaction, a consumer provides a check to a payee and information from the check is used to initiate a one-time EFT from the consumer's account. Although transfers originated by checks are not covered by Regulation E, an ECK is treated as an EFT and not a payment originated by check. Payees must obtain the consumer's authorization for each ECK transaction. A consumer authorizes a one-time EFT for an ECK transaction when the consumer receives notice that the transaction will or may be processed as an EFT and goes forward with the underlying transaction[2] (sections 205.3(b)(2)(i) and (ii) and staff commentary 205.3(b)(2)–3).

Before December 31, 2009, a person using the check to initiate the EFT had to include a notice that funds may be withdrawn from the consumer's account as soon as the same day payment is received, and, as applicable, that the consumer's check will not be returned by the financial institution (section 205.3(b)(2)(iii) and appendix A–6). This requirement is no longer in effect. If a payee re-presents electronically a check that has been returned unpaid, the transaction is not an EFT, and Regulation E does not apply because the transaction originated by check (staff commentary 205.3(c)(1)–1)).

Regulation E, however, applies to a fee collected electronically from a consumer's account for a check or EFT returned unpaid. A consumer authorizes a one-time EFT from the consumer's account to pay the fee for the returned item or transfer if the person collecting the fee provides notice to the consumer stating the amount of the fee and that the person may electronically collect the fee, and the consumer goes forward with the underlying transaction[3] (section 205.3(b)(3)). These authorization requirements do not apply to fees imposed by the account-holding financial institution for returning the check or EFT or paying the amount of an overdraft (staff commentary 205.3(b)(3)–1)).

II. Disclosures

Disclosures, Generally–Section 205.4

Required disclosures must be clear and readily understandable, in writing, and in a form the consumer may keep. The required disclosures may be provided to the consumer in electronic form, if the consumer affirmatively

---

[2] For POS transactions, the notice must be posted in a prominent and conspicuous location and a copy of the notice must be provided to the consumer at the time of the transaction (sections 205.3(b)(2)(i) and (ii) and staff commentary 205.3(b)(2)–3).

[3] For POS transactions, the notice must be posted in a prominent and conspicuous location, and a copy of the notice must either be provided to the consumer at the time of the transaction or mailed to the consumer's address as soon as reasonably practicable after the person initiates the EFT to collect the fee (section 205.3(b)(3)).

consents after receiving a notice that complies with the Electronic Signatures in Global and National Commerce Act of 2000 (E-Sign Act) (section 205.4(a)(1)).

Disclosures may be made in a language other than English, if the disclosures are made available in English upon the consumer's request (section 205.4(a)(2)).

A financial institution has the option of disclosing additional information and combining disclosures required by other laws (for example, Truth in Lending Act disclosures) with Regulation E disclosures (section 205.4(b)).

A financial institution may combine required disclosures into a single statement if a consumer holds two or more accounts at the financial institution. Thus, a single periodic statement or error resolution notice is sufficient for multiple accounts. In addition, it is only necessary for a financial institution to provide one set of disclosures for a joint account (section 205.4(c)(l) and (2)).

Two or more financial institutions that jointly provide EFT services may contract among themselves to meet the requirements that the regulation imposes on any or all of them. When making initial disclosures (section 205.7) and disclosures of a change in terms or an error resolution notice (section 205.8), a financial institution in a shared system only needs to make disclosures that are within its knowledge and apply to its relationship with the consumer for whom it holds an account (section 205.4(d)).

Initial Disclosure of Terms and Conditions–Section 205.7

A financial institution must provide initial disclosures of the terms and conditions of EFT services before the first EFT is made or at the time the consumer contracts for an EFT service. It must give a summary of various consumer rights under the regulation, including the consumer's liability for unauthorized EFTs, the types of EFTs the consumer may make, limits on the frequency or dollar amount, fees charged by the financial institution, and the error-resolution procedures. Appendix A to part 205 provides model clauses that financial institutions may use to provide the disclosures.

Timing of disclosures. A financial institution must make the required disclosures at the time a consumer contracts for an electronic fund transfer service or before the first electronic fund transfer is made involving the consumer's account (section 205.7(a)).

Disclosures given by a financial institution earlier than the regulation requires (for example, when the consumer opens a checking account) need not be repeated when the consumer later authorizes an ECK or agrees with a third party to initiate preauthorized transfers to or from the consumer's account, unless the terms and conditions differ from the previously disclosed term. This interpretation also applies to any notice provided about one-time EFTs from a consumer's account initiated using information from the consumer's check. On the other hand, if an agreement for EFT services to be provided by an account-holding financial institution is directly between the consumer and the account-holding financial institution, disclosures must be given in close proximity to the event requiring disclosure, for example, when the consumer contracts for a new service (staff commentary 205.7(a)–1).

When a consumer authorizes a third party to debit or credit the consumer's account, an account-holding financial institution that has not received advance notice of the transfer or transfers must provide the required disclosures as soon as reasonably possible after the first debit or credit is made, unless the financial institution has previously given the disclosures (staff commentary 205.7(a)–2).

If a consumer opens a new account permitting EFTs at a financial institution, and the consumer has already received Regulation E disclosures for another account at that financial institution, the financial institution need only disclose terms and conditions that differ from those previously given (staff commentary 205.7(a)–3).

If a financial institution joins an interchange or shared network system (which provides access to terminals operated by other financial institutions), disclosures are required for additional EFT services not previously available to consumers if the terms and conditions differ from those previously disclosed (staff commentary 205.7(a)–4).

A financial institution may provide disclosures covering all EFT services that it offers, even if some consumers have not arranged to use all services (staff commentary 205.7(a)–5).

Addition of EFT services. A financial institution must make disclosures for any new EFT service added to a consumer's account if the terms and conditions are different from those described in the initial disclosures. ECK transactions may be a new type of transfer requiring new disclosures (appendix A–2 and staff commentary 205.7(c)–1).

Content of disclosures. Section 205.7(b) requires a financial institution to provide the following disclosures as they apply:

- **Liability of consumers for unauthorized electronic fund transfers.** The financial institution must include a summary of the consumer's liability (under section 205.6, state law, or other applicable law or agreement) for unauthorized transfers (section 205.7(b)(1)). A financial institution does not need to provide the liability disclosures if it imposes no liability. If it later decides to impose liability, it must first provide the disclosures (staff commentary 205.7(b)(1)–1). The financial institution can choose to include advice on promptly reporting unauthorized transfers or the loss or theft of the access device (staff commentary 205.7(b)(1)–3).
- **Telephone number and address.** A financial institution must provide a specific telephone number and address, on or with the disclosure statement, for reporting a lost or stolen access device or a possible unauthorized transfer (staff commentary 205.7(b)(2)–2). Except for the telephone number and address for reporting a lost or stolen access device or a possible unauthorized transfer, the disclosure may insert a reference to a telephone number that is readily available to the consumer, such as "Call your branch office. The number is shown on your periodic statement" (staff commentary 205.7(b)(2)–2).
- **Business days.** The financial institution's business days (section 205.7(b)(3)).
- **Types of transfers and limitations on frequency or dollar amount.** Limitations on the frequency and dollar amount of transfers generally must be disclosed in detail (section 205.7(b)(4)). If the confidentiality of certain details is essential to the security of an account or system, these details may be withheld (but the fact that limitations exist must still be disclosed).[4] A limitation on account activity that restricts the consumer's ability to make EFTs must be disclosed even if the restriction also applies to transfers made by non-electronic means. Financial institutions are not required to list preauthorized transfers among the types of transfers that a consumer can make (staff commentary 205.7(b)(4)–3). Financial

---

[4] For example, if a financial institution limits cash ATM withdrawals to $100 per day, the financial institution may disclose that daily withdrawal limitations apply and need not disclose that the limitations may not always be in force (such as during periods when its ATMs are off–line) (staff commentary 205.7(b)(4)–1).

institutions must disclose that one-time EFTs initiated using information from a consumer's check are among the types of transfers that a consumer can make (appendix A–2 and staff commentary 205.7(b)(4)–4).

- **Fees.** A financial institution must disclose all fees for EFTs or for the right to make EFTs (section 205.7(b)(5)). Other fees, for example, minimum-balance fees, stop-payment fees, account overdrafts, or ATM inquiry fees, may, but need not, be disclosed under Regulation E (Regulation DD, 12 CFR part 230) (staff commentary 205.7(b)(5)–1). A per-item fee for EFTs must be disclosed even if the same fee is imposed on non-electronic transfers. If a per-item fee is imposed only under certain conditions, such as when the transactions in the cycle exceed a certain number, those conditions must be disclosed. Itemization of the various fees may be on the disclosure statement or on an accompanying document referenced in the statement (staff commentary 205.7(b)(5)–2).

- **Networks.** A financial institution must disclose that a network used to complete the EFT, as well as an ATM operator, may charge a fee for an EFT or for balance inquiries (section 205.7(b)(11)).

- **Documentation.** A summary of the consumer's right to receipts and periodic statements, as provided in section 205.9, and notices regarding preauthorized transfers, as provided in sections 205.10(a) and 205.10(d) (section 205.7(b)(6)).

- **Stop payment.** A summary of the consumer's right to stop payment of a preauthorized electronic fund transfer and the procedure for placing a stop-payment order, as provided in section 205.10(c) (section 205.7(b)(7)).

- **Liability of institution.** A summary of the financial institution's liability to the consumer under section 910 of the EFTA for failure to make or to stop certain transfers (section 205.7(b)(8)).

- **Confidentiality.** The circumstances under which, in the ordinary course of business, the financial institution may provide information concerning the consumer's account to third parties (section 205.7(b)(9)). A financial institution must describe the circumstances under which any information relating to an account to or from which EFTs are permitted will be made available to third parties, not just information concerning those EFTs. Third parties include other subsidiaries of the same holding company (staff commentary 205.7(b)(9)–1).

- **Error resolution.** The error-resolution notice must be substantially similar to Model Form A–3 in appendix A of part 205. A financial institution may use different wording so long as the substance of the notice remains the same, may delete inapplicable provisions (for example, the requirement for written confirmation of an oral notification), and may substitute substantive state law requirements affording greater consumer protection than Regulation E (staff commentary 205.7(b)(10)–1). To take advantage of the longer time periods for resolving errors under section 205.11(c)(3) (for new accounts as defined in Regulation CC, transfers initiated outside the United States, or transfers resulting from POS debit card transactions), a financial institution must have disclosed these longer time periods. Similarly, a financial institution relying on the exception from provisional crediting in section 205.11(c)(2) for accounts relating to extensions of credit by securities brokers and dealers (Regulation T, 12 CFR 220) must disclose accordingly (staff commentary 205.7(b)(10)–2).

Change in Terms; Error Resolution Notice–Section 205.8

If a financial institution contemplates a change in terms, it must mail or deliver a written or electronic notice to the consumer at least 21 days before the effective date of any change in a term or condition required to be disclosed under section 205.7(b) if the change would result in any of the following:

- Increased fees or charges,
- Increased liability for the consumer,
- Fewer types of available EFTs, or
- Stricter limitations on the frequency or dollar amounts of transfers (section 205.8(a)(1)).

If an immediate change in terms or conditions is necessary to maintain or restore the security of an EFT system or account, the financial institution does not need to give prior notice. If the change is to be permanent, however, the financial institution must provide notice in writing of the change to the consumer on or with the next regularly scheduled periodic statement or within 30 days, unless disclosures would jeopardize the security of the system or account (section 205.8(a)(2)).

For accounts to or from which EFTs can be made, the financial institution must mail, deliver, or provide electronically to the consumer at least once each calendar year, the error resolution notice in 12 CFR 205 appendix A–Model Form A–3, or one substantially similar. Alternatively, the financial institution may include an abbreviated error resolution notice substantially similar to the notice set out in appendix A (Model Form A–3) with each periodic statement (section 205.8(b)).

Disclosures at ATMs–Section 205.16

An ATM operator that charges a fee is required to post notice that a fee will be imposed and disclose the amount of the fee (section 205.16(b)). Notices must be posted (1) in a prominent and conspicuous location on or at the machine and (2) on the screen or on a paper notice before the consumer is committed to paying a fee (section 205.16(c)(1) and (2)). The fee may be imposed by the ATM operator only if (1) the consumer is provided the required notices and (2) the consumer elects to continue the transaction after receiving the required disclosures (section 205.16(e)).

The "prominent and conspicuous notice" standard applies to a notice posted on or at the ATM. The "clear and readily understandable standard" applies to the content of the notice. The requirement that the notice be in a retainable format only applies to printed notices (not those on the ATM screen) (section 205.16(c)).

These fee disclosures are not required when a network owner is not charging a fee directly to the consumer; for example, some network owners charge an interchange fee to financial institutions whose customers use the network (staff commentary 205.7(b)(5)–3). If the network practices change such that the network charges the consumer directly, these fee disclosure requirements would apply to the network (section 205.7(c)).

Overdraft Service Disclosures–Section 205.17

Disclosure requirements for overdraft services are addressed in section III of this booklet.

Gift Card Disclosures–Section 205.20(c)

Disclosures must be clear and conspicuous and generally in a written or electronic form (except for certain pre-purchase disclosures, which may be given orally) that the consumer may retain. The fees, terms, and conditions of expiration required to be disclosed before purchase may not be changed after purchase.

A number of disclosures must be made on the actual card. Making such disclosures in an accompanying terms and conditions document, on packaging surrounding a certificate or card, or on a sticker or other label affixed to the certificate or card does not constitute a disclosure on the certificate or card. Those disclosures include the following:

- The existence, amount, and frequency of any dormancy, inactivity, or service fee;
- The expiration date for the underlying funds (or the fact that the funds do not expire);
- A toll-free telephone number and (if any) a Web site that the consumer may use to obtain a replacement certificate or card if the certificate or card expires while underlying funds are still available;
- A statement that the certificate or card expires, but the underlying funds do not expire or expire later than the certificate or card, as well as a statement that the consumer may contact the issuer for a replacement card;[5] and
- A toll-free telephone number and (if any) a Web site that the consumer may use to obtain information about fees.

Additional disclosure requirements regarding fees. In addition to the disclosure requirements related to dormancy, inactivity, or service fees, all other fees must be disclosed as well. These disclosures must be provided on or with the certificate or card and disclosed before purchase. The certificate or card must also disclose a toll-free telephone number and Web site, if one is maintained, that a consumer may use to obtain fee information or replacement certificates or cards (section 205.20(f)).

Disclosure Requirements for Loyalty, Award, or Promotional Gift Cards–Section 205.20(a)(4)

To qualify for the exclusion for loyalty, award, or promotional gift cards, the following must be disclosed:

- A statement indicating that the card, code, or other device is issued for loyalty, award, or promotional purposes, which must be included on the front of the card, code, or other device;
- The expiration date for the underlying funds, which must be included on the front of the card, code, or other device;
- The amount of any fees that may be imposed in connection with the card, code, or other device, and the conditions under which they may be

---

[5] This requirement does not apply to non-reloadable certificates or cards that expire seven years or more after the date of manufacture.

imposed, which must be provided on or with the card, code, or other device; and

- A toll-free telephone number and, if one is maintained, a Web site, that a consumer may use to obtain fee information, which must be included on the card, code, or other device.

III. Electronic Transaction Overdraft Services Opt-In

Background. In recent years, overdraft protection services have been extended to cover overdrafts resulting from non-check transactions, including ATM withdrawals, debit card transactions at POS, online transactions, preauthorized transfers, and ACH transactions. Generally, institutions charge a flat fee each time an overdraft is paid, although some institutions have a tiered fee structure and charge higher fees based on the amount of the negative balance at the end of the day or as the number of overdrafts increases. Institutions commonly charge the same amount for paying check and ACH overdrafts as they would if they returned the item unpaid. Some institutions also impose a fee for each day the account remains overdrawn. For debit card overdrafts, the dollar amount of the fee and multiple assessments can exceed the dollar amount of the overdrafts.

In 2005, the Office of the Comptroller of the Currency (OCC), the Board of Governors of the Federal Reserve System (Board), the Federal Deposit Insurance Corporation, and the National Credit Union Administration (the agencies) issued guidance concerning the marketing, disclosure, and implementation of overdraft programs. The guidance also covers safety and soundness considerations and establishes a number of best practices financial institutions should incorporate into their overdraft programs. The 2009 revisions to Regulation E supersede portions of the guidance related to ATM and one-time debit card overdraft transactions. In addition to the revised Regulation E requirements, however, institutions are again advised to incorporate the Joint Guidance on Overdraft Protection Programs (*see* OCC 2005--9, April 6, 2005) into their overdraft protection programs.

Section 205.17 was added in the 2009 revision to Regulation E.[6] The revision provides consumers with a choice to opt into their institution's overdraft protection program and be charged a fee for overdrafts for ATM and one-time debit card transactions. It also requires disclosure of the fees and terms associated with the institution's overdraft service. Before an institution may

---

[6] 74 FR 59033, November 17, 2009; 75 FR 31665, June 4, 2010.

assess overdraft fees, the consumer must opt in, or affirmatively consent, to the overdraft service for ATM and one-time debit card transactions, and the consumer has an ongoing right to revoke consent. Institutions may not require an opt-in for ATM and one-time debit transactions as a condition to the payment of overdrafts for checks and other transactions. The account terms, conditions and features must be the same for consumers who opt in and for those who do not.

Opt-in requirement for overdraft services. The financial institution may assess a fee for paying an ATM or one-time debit card transaction pursuant to an overdraft service only if it has met the following requirements:

- The financial institution has provided the consumer with a written (or, if the consumer agrees, electronic) notice, segregated from all other information, describing the overdraft service;
- The financial institution has provided a reasonable opportunity for the consumer to affirmatively consent (opt in) to the overdraft service for ATM and one-time debit card transactions;
- The financial institution has obtained the consumer's affirmative consent (opt in) for ATM and one-time debit card transactions; and
- The financial institution has mailed or delivered written (or, if the consumer agrees, electronic) confirmation of the consent, including a statement informing the consumer of the right to revoke consent. An institution complies if it adopts reasonable procedures to ensure that it assesses overdraft fees only for transactions paid after mailing or delivering the confirmation to the consumer (section 205.17(b)(1); staff commentary 205.17(b)–7)).

Fee prohibitions. As a general rule, an institution may not charge overdraft fees for paying an ATM or one-time debit card transaction unless the consumer has opted in. The fee prohibition also applies to an institution that has a policy and practice of not paying an ATM or one-time debit card overdraft when it reasonably believes at the time of the authorization request that the consumer does not have sufficient funds available to pay the transaction, although the institution does not have to comply with the notice and opt-in requirements (staff commentary 205.17(b)–1(iv)).

Lack of consent does not prohibit the financial institution from paying ATM or one-time debit card overdrafts. The financial institution, however, may charge a fee only if the consumer has consented to the institution's overdraft service for ATM and one-time debit card transactions (staff commentary 205.17(b)–

2). Conversely, the financial institution is not required to pay an ATM or one-time debit card overdraft even if the consumer has consented to pay a fee (staff commentary 205.17(b)–3).

For a consumer who has not opted in, if a fee or charge is based on the amount of the outstanding negative balance, an institution may not charge a fee for a negative balance that is solely attributable to an ATM or one-time debit card transaction. An institution may assess a fee, however, if the negative balance is attributable in whole or in part to a check, ACH transaction, or other type of transaction not subject to the prohibition on assessing overdraft fees (staff commentary 205.17(b)–8).

For a consumer who has not opted in, the institution may not assess daily or sustained negative balance, overdraft, or similar fees for a negative balance, based solely on ATM or one-time debit card transactions. If the negative balance is attributable in part to a check, ACH transaction, or other type of transaction not subject to the prohibition on assessing overdraft fees, however, the institution may charge a daily or sustained overdraft or similar fee, even if the consumer has not opted in. The date the fee may be charged is based on the date on which the check, ACH, or other type of transaction is paid into overdraft (staff commentary 205.17(b)–9).

Contents and format of notice. The notice describing the overdraft service must be substantially similar to Model Form A–9. The notice must include all of the following items, and may not contain any other information not expressly specified or otherwise permitted:

- A brief description of the overdraft service and the types of transactions for which the financial institution may charge a fee;
- The dollar amount of any fee that may be charged for an ATM or one-time debit card transaction, including any daily or other overdraft fees;[7]
- The maximum number of fees that may be charged per day, or, if applicable, that there is no limit;
- An explanation of the right to affirmatively consent to the overdraft

---

[7] If the amount of the fee may vary based on the number of times the consumer has overdrawn the account, the amount of the overdraft, or other factors, the financial institution must disclose the maximum fee.

service, including the methods by which the consumer may consent;[8] and

- The availability of a line of credit or a service that transfers funds from another account to cover overdrafts, if the financial institution offers those alternatives[9] (section 205.17(d)(1) through (d)(5)).

The financial institution also may (but is not required to) include the following information, to the extent applicable:

- Disclosure of the right to opt into, or out of, the payment of overdrafts for other types of transactions (e.g., checks, ACH transactions, or automatic bill payments) and a means for the consumer to exercise such choices;
- Disclosure of the financial institution's returned item fee, as well as the fact that merchants may charge additional fees; and
- Disclosure of the right to revoke consent (section 205.17(d)(6)).

Reasonable opportunity to consent. The financial institution must provide a reasonable opportunity to consent. Reasonable methods of consent include mail, if the financial institution provides a form for the consumer to fill out and mail; telephone, if the financial institution provides a readily available telephone line that the consumer may call; electronic means, if the financial institution provides a form that can be accessed and processed at its Web site, by which means the consumer may click on a box to consent and click on a button to affirm consent; or in person, if the financial institution provides a form for the consumer to complete and present at a branch or office (staff commentary 205.17(b)–4). The financial institution may provide the opportunity to consent and require the consumer to make a choice as a step to opening an account (staff commentary 205.17(b)–5).

Affirmative consent is necessary. An important feature of the opt-in is that the consumer's affirmative consent is necessary before the institution may charge overdraft fees for paying an ATM or one-time debit card transaction

---

[8] Institutions may tailor the response portion of Model Form A–9 to the methods offered. For example, a tear-off portion of Model Form A–9 is not necessary if consumers may only opt-in by telephone or electronically (staff commentary 205.17(d)–3).

[9] If the institution offers both a line of credit subject to the Board's Regulation Z (12 CFR 226) and a service that transfers funds from another account of the consumer held at the institution to cover overdrafts, the institution must state in its opt-in notice that both alternative plans are offered. If the institution offers one, but not the other, it must state in its opt-in notice the alternative plan that it offers. If the institution does not offer either plan, it should omit the reference to the alternative plans. (staff commentary 205.17(d)–5). If the financial institution offers additional alternatives for paying overdrafts, it may (but is not required to) disclose those alternatives (staff commentary 205.17(d)(5)).

(section 205.17(b)(1)(iii)). The consent must be separate from other consents or acknowledgments (including consent to receive disclosures electronically). Check boxes are allowed, but the check box and the consumer's signature may only apply to the consumer's consent to opt-in. Preprinted disclosures about the overdraft service provided with a signature card or contract do not constitute affirmative consent (staff commentary 205.17(b)–6).

Confirmation and consumer's right to revoke. Not only must the consumer affirmatively consent, but the institution must also mail or deliver to the consumer a written confirmation (or electronic, if the consumer agrees) that the consumer has consented, along with a statement informing the consumer of the right to revoke the consent at any time (section 205.17(b)(1)(iv) and staff commentary 205.17(b)–7). An institution complies with the confirmation requirement if it has adopted reasonable procedures to ensure that overdraft fees are assessed only on transactions paid after the confirmation is mailed or delivered to the consumer (staff commentary 205.17(b)–7).

Assessing fees. For consumers who have not opted in, institutions are prohibited from charging overdraft fees for paying those transactions. This prohibition applies to daily or sustained overdraft, negative balance, or similar fees. The rule does not, however, prohibit an institution from assessing these fees if the negative balance is attributable, in whole or part, to a check, ACH, or other transaction not subject to the fee prohibition. If, for example, the negative balance is attributable in part to an ATM transaction, and in part to a check, a fee may be assessed based on the date when the check is paid into overdraft, not the date of the ATM or one-time debit transaction (staff commentary 205.17(b)–9).

Conditioning payment of other overdrafts. The financial institution may not condition the payment of other types of overdraft transactions on the consumer's affirmative consent, and the financial institution may not decline to pay other types of overdraft transactions because the consumer has not affirmatively consented to the payment of ATM and one-time debit card overdrafts (section 205.17(b)(2)). In other words, the financial institution may not use different criteria for paying other types of overdraft transactions for consumers who have consented and for consumers who have not consented (staff commentary 205.17(b)(2)–1).

Same account terms, conditions, and features. The financial institution must provide to consumers who do not affirmatively consent to the same account terms, conditions, and features (except the payment of ATM and one-time debit overdrafts) that are available to consumers who do affirmatively consent (section 205.17(b)(3)). That requirement includes, but is not limited to, the following:

- Interest rates paid
- Fees assessed
- The type of ATM or debit card provided to the depositor[10]
- Minimum balance requirements
- Online bill payment services (staff commentary 205.17(b)(3)–1)

Joint accounts. Any consumer may consent, or revoke consent, for payment of ATM or one-time debit card transactions from a joint account (section 205.17(e)).

Continuing right to consent or revoke. A consumer may consent to the payment of ATM and one-time debit card overdrafts at any time. A consumer may also revoke consent at any time. The financial institution must implement a revocation as soon as reasonably practicable (section 205.17(f)). The financial institution need not waive overdraft fees assessed before it implements the consumer's revocation (staff commentary 205.17(f)–1).

Duration of consent. Consent remains effective until the consumer revokes it, unless the financial institution terminates the overdraft service (section 205.17(g)). The financial institution may terminate the overdraft service, for example, if the consumer makes excessive use of the service (staff commentary 205.17(g)–1).

Effective date. The overdraft services rule became effective on January 19, 2010, and compliance became mandatory starting July 1, 2010. For accounts opened on or after July 1, 2010, the financial institution must obtain consent before charging a fee for payment of any ATM or one-time debit overdraft. For accounts opened before July 1, 2010, however, the financial institution may not charge a fee for paying any ATM or one-time debit overdraft on or after August 15, 2010, unless it has obtained consent. (section 205.17(c)).

---

[10] For example, the financial institution may not provide a PIN-only debit card to consumers who do not opt in and a debit card with both PIN and signature-debit features to consumers who do opt in.

IV. Issuance of Access Devices

In general, a financial institution may issue an access device to a consumer only in the following cases:

- The consumer requested it in writing or orally.[11]
- It is a renewal of, or a substitute for, an accepted access device (as defined in section 205.2(a)) (section 205.5(a)).

Only one renewal or substitute device may replace a previously issued device. A financial institution may provide additional devices at the time it issues the renewal or substitute access device provided the institution complies with the requirements for issuing unsolicited access devices for the additional devices (staff commentaries 205.5(a)(2)–1 and 205.5(b)–5).

A financial institution may issue an unsolicited access device only if the access device meets all of the following criteria. The access device is

- not validated, that is, it cannot be used to initiate an EFT.
- accompanied by the explanation that it is not validated and how the consumer may dispose of it if the consumer does not wish to validate it.
- accompanied by a complete disclosure, in accordance with section 205.7, of the consumer's rights and liabilities that will apply if the access device is validated.
- validated only upon oral or written request from the consumer and after a verification of the consumer's identity by some reasonable means (section 205.5(b)).

The financial institution may use any reasonable means of verifying the consumer's identity, but the consumer is not liable for any unauthorized transfers if an imposter succeeds in validating the access device (staff commentary 205.5(b)–4).

Payroll card access devices. Consistent with section 205.5(a), a financial institution may issue a payroll card access device only in response to an oral or written request for the device or as a renewal or substitute for an accepted access device. A consumer is deemed to request an access device for a

---

[11] For a joint account, a financial institution may issue an access device to each account holder for whom the requesting holder specifically requests an access device (staff commentary 205.5(a)(1)–1).

payroll account when the consumer chooses to receive salary or other compensation through a payroll card account (staff commentary 205.18(a)–1).

EFT added to credit card. The EFTA and Regulation E apply when the capability to initiate EFTs is added to an accepted credit card (as defined under Regulation Z). The EFTA and Regulation E also apply to the issuance of an access device that permits credit extensions under a pre-existing agreement between the consumer and a financial institution to extend credit only to cover overdrafts (or to maintain a specified minimum balance). The Truth in Lending Act and Regulation Z govern the addition of a credit feature to an accepted access device, and, except as discussed above, the issuance of a credit card that is also an access device. For information on Regulation E's relationship to other laws, including the Truth in Lending Act, see section 205.12.

V. Consumer Liability and Error Resolution

Liability of Consumers for Unauthorized Transfers–Section 205.6

A consumer may be liable for an unauthorized EFT (defined in section 205.2(m)) depending on when the consumer notifies the financial institution and whether an access device was used to conduct the transaction. Under the EFTA, there is no bright-line time limit within which consumers must report unauthorized EFTs (71 Fed. Reg. 1638, 1653 (January 10, 2006)).

The extent of the consumer's liability is determined solely by the consumer's promptness in notifying the financial institution (staff commentary 205.6(b)–3). Other factors may not be used as a basis to hold consumers liable. Regulation E expressly prohibits the following factors as the basis for imposing greater liability than is permissible under Regulation E: the consumer was negligent (for example, by writing a PIN on an ATM card); an agreement between the consumer and the financial institution provides for greater liability; or the consumer is liable for a greater amount under state law (staff commentaries 205.6(b)–2 and 205.6(b)–3).

A consumer may only be held liable for an unauthorized transaction, within the limitations set forth in section 205.6(b), if

- the financial institution has provided all of the following written disclosures to the consumer:
  - A summary of the consumer's liability for unauthorized EFTs.

- The telephone number and address for reporting that an unauthorized EFT has been or may be made.
- The financial institution's business days.
- Any access device used to affect the EFT was an accepted access device (as defined in section 205.2(a)).
- The financial institution has provided a means to identify the consumer to whom the access device was issued (section 205.6(a)).

Regulation E allows, but does not require, the financial institution to provide a separate means to identify each consumer of a multiple-user account (staff commentary 205.6(a)–2).

The limitations on the amount of consumer liability for unauthorized EFTs, the time limits within which consumers must report unauthorized EFTs, and the liability for failing to adhere to those time limits, are listed in the following chart. The financial institution may impose less consumer liability than is provided by section 205.6 based on state law or the deposit agreement (section 205.6(b)(6)).

Consumer Liability for Unauthorized Transfers:
Electronic Fund Transfer Act—Regulation E (12 CFR 205.6)

Event	Timing of consumer notice to financial institution	Maximum liability
Loss or theft of access device[a]	Within two business days after learning of loss or theft.	Lesser of $50, OR total amount of unauthorized transfers.
Loss or theft of access device	More than two business days after learning of loss or theft up to 60 calendar days after transmittal of statement showing first unauthorized transfer made with access device.	Lesser of $500, OR the sum of (a) $50 or the total amount of unauthorized transfers occurring in the first two business days, whichever is less, AND (b) the amount of unauthorized transfers occurring after two business days and before notice to the financial institution.[b]
Loss or theft of access device	More than 60 calendar days after transmittal of statement showing first unauthorized transfer made with access device.	For transfers occurring within the 60-day period, the lesser of $500, OR the sum of (a) lesser of $50 or the amount of unauthorized transfers in first two business days, AND (b) the amount of unauthorized transfers occurring after two business days. For transfers occurring after the 60-day period, unlimited liability (until the financial institution is notified).[c]
Unauthorized transfer(s) not involving loss or theft of an access device	Within 60 calendar days after transmittal of the periodic statement on which the unauthorized transfer first appears.	No liability.
Unauthorized transfer(s) not involving loss or theft of an access device	More than 60 calendar days after transmittal of the periodic statement on which the unauthorized transfer first appears.	Unlimited liability for unauthorized transfers occurring 60 calendar days after the periodic statement and before notice to the financial institution.

[a] Includes a personal identification number if used without a card in a telephone transaction, for example.

[b] Provided the financial institution demonstrates that these transfers would not have occurred had notice been given within the two-business-day period.

[c] Provided the financial institution demonstrates that these transfers would not have occurred had notice been given within the 60-day period.

Knowledge of loss or theft. The fact that a consumer has received a periodic statement reflecting an unauthorized transaction is a factor, but not conclusive evidence, in determining whether the consumer had knowledge of a loss or theft of the access device (staff commentary 205.6(b)(1)–2).

Timing of notice. If a consumer's delay in notifying a financial institution was due to extenuating circumstances, such as extended travel or hospitalization, the time periods for notification specified above must be extended to a reasonable time (section 205.6(b)(4); staff commentary 205.6(b)(4)–1).

Notice to the financial institution. A consumer gives notice to a financial institution about unauthorized use when the consumer takes reasonable steps to provide the financial institution with the pertinent information, whether or not a particular employee actually receives the information (section 205.6(b)(5)(i)). Even if the consumer is unable to provide the account number or the card number, the notice effectively limits the consumer's liability if the consumer sufficiently identifies the account in question, for example, by giving the name on the account and the type of account (staff commentary 205.6(b)(5)–3). At the consumer's option, notice may be given in person, by telephone, or in writing (section 205.6(b)(5)(ii)). Notice in writing is considered given at the time the consumer mails the notice or delivers the notice for transmission by any other usual means to the financial institution. Notice may also be considered given when the financial institution becomes aware of circumstances leading to the reasonable belief that an unauthorized transfer has been or may be made (section 205.6(b)(5)(iii)).

Relation of error resolution to truth in lending. Regulation E's liability and error resolution provisions apply to an extension of credit that occurs under an agreement between the consumer and a financial institution to extend credit when the consumer's account is overdrawn, to maintain a specified minimum balance in the consumer's account, or under an overdraft service (section 205.12(a)(1)(ii)). As provided in section 205.12 and related commentary, for transactions involving access devices that also function as credit cards, the liability and error resolution provisions of Regulation E or Regulation Z will apply depending on the nature of the transaction:

- If the unauthorized use of a combined access device/credit card solely involves an extension of credit, other than an extension of credit described under section 205.12(a)(1)(iii), and does not involve an EFT, for example, when the card is used to draw cash advances directly from a credit line, only the error resolution provisions of Regulation Z will apply.

- If the unauthorized use of a combined access device/credit card involves only an EFT, for example, debit card purchases or cash withdrawals at an ATM from a checking account, only the error resolution provisions of Regulation E will apply.
- If a combined access device/credit card is stolen and unauthorized transactions are made by using the card as both a debit card and a credit card, Regulation E will apply to the unauthorized transactions in which the card was used as a debit card, and Regulation Z will apply to the unauthorized transactions in which the card was used as a credit card.

Procedures for Resolving Errors–Section 205.11

This section defines the term **error** and describes the steps the consumer must take when asserting an error in order to receive the protection of the EFTA and Regulation E and the procedures that a financial institution must follow to resolve an alleged error.

An **error** includes any of the following:

- An unauthorized EFT.
- An incorrect EFT to or from the consumer's account.
- The omission from a periodic statement of an EFT to or from the consumer's account that should have been included.
- A computational or bookkeeping error made by the financial institution relating to an EFT.
- The consumer's receipt of an incorrect amount of money from an electronic terminal.
- An EFT not identified in accordance with the requirements of sections 205.9 or 205.10(a).
- A consumer's request for any documentation required by sections 205.9 or 205.10(a) or for additional information or clarification concerning an EFT (section 205.11(a)(1)).

The term **error** does not include

- A routine inquiry about the balance in the consumer's account or a request for duplicate copies of documentation or other information that is made only for tax or other record-keeping purposes (sections 205.11(a)(2)(i), (ii), and (iii)).

- The fact that a financial institution does not make a terminal receipt available for a transfer of $15 or less in accordance with 205.9(e) (staff commentary 205.11(a)–6).

A financial institution must comply with the error resolution procedures in section 205.11 with respect to any oral or written notice of error from the consumer that

- the financial institution receives not later than 60 days after sending a periodic statement or other documentation first reflecting the alleged error (205.14 and 205.18).
- enables the financial institution to identify the consumer's name and account number.
- indicates why the consumer believes the error exists and, to the extent possible, the type, date, and amount of the error (section 205.11(b)(1)).

A financial institution may require a consumer to give written confirmation of an error within 10 business days of giving oral notice. The financial institution must provide the address where confirmation must be sent (section 205.11(b)(2)).

Section 909(b) of the EFTA establishes that the burden of proof is on the financial institution to show that the transaction was authorized. Conducting good faith, reasonable investigations can help institutions satisfy this burden of proof. The EFTA provides for treble damages in legal actions filed by consumers if certain factual circumstances are present.

The OCC is concerned that some institutions may be rejecting claims of unauthorized transactions solely because the customer's ATM card or debit card and PIN were used in the transaction, and the customer supplied no information indicating that the card or PIN was misappropriated. These facts alone may be insufficient to establish that a transaction was authorized because fraudulent means may have been used to obtain the customer's account number, card, or PIN. For instance, the customer may have been a victim of "shoulder surfing," a practice used by criminals to obtain account or card numbers or PINs by observing customer transactions. Therefore, institutions cannot assume that they have satisfied their duty to investigate simply by concluding that the customer's debit card and PIN were used in the transaction at issue. Rather, institutions must take steps to investigate whether there are indications that unauthorized use occurred.

To assist institutions in complying with EFTA and Regulation E error resolution procedures, the OCC has compiled a list of actions banks and thrifts may take to help determine whether a transaction was authorized.[12] A reasonable investigation under Regulation E might include review of one or more of the following items:

- Documentation or written, signed statements provided by the customer.
- Historical information on the customer's pattern of use (e.g., time, frequency, location, and types and amounts of transactions).
- Location of the transaction in relation to the customer's residence, place of business, or normal shopping locations.
- Customer's location at the time of the unauthorized transaction.
- Problems reported by other customers regarding the access device or ATM.
- Signature information on POS transactions.
- Police reports, if available.
- Film from security cameras, if available.

An institution may request a customer's reasonable cooperation in any such investigation. It may not, however, deny a claim of error based solely on the cardholder's failure to comply with such a request.

Error resolution procedures. After receiving a notice of error, the financial institution must do all of the following:

- Promptly investigate the oral or written allegation of error.
- Complete its investigation within 10 business days (section 205.11(c)(1)).
- Report the results of its investigation within three business days after completing its investigation.
- Correct the error within one business day after determining that an error has occurred.

The financial institution may take up to 45 calendar days (section 205.11(c)(2)) to complete its investigation provided it

- provisionally credits the funds (including interest, where applicable) to the consumer's account within the 10 business-day period.

---

[12] As a general matter, a financial institution may limit its review to its own records if (1) the transfer is to or from a third party, and (2) there is no agreement between the institution and the third party for the type of electronic fund transfer involved (12 CFR 205.11(c)(4).

- advises the consumer within two business days of the provisional crediting.
- gives the consumer full use of the funds during the investigation.

A financial institution need not provisionally credit the account to take up to 45 calendar days to complete its investigation if the consumer fails to provide the required written confirmation of an oral notice of error or if the notice of error involves an account subject to the margin requirements or other aspects of Regulation T (Securities Credit by Brokers and Dealers, 12 CFR 220) (section 205.11(c)(2)(i)(B)).

When an error involves an unauthorized EFT, however, the financial institution must comply with the requirements of the provisions relating to unauthorized EFTs before holding the consumer liable, even if the consumer does not provide a notice of error within the time limits in section 205.11(b) (staff commentary 205.11(b)(1)–7).

When investigating a claim of error, the financial institution need only review its own records if the alleged error concerns a transfer to or from a third party and there is no agreement between the financial institution and the third party for the type of EFT involved (section 205.11(c)(4)). The financial institution may not limit its investigation solely to the payment instructions when other information within the financial institution's records pertaining to a particular account may help to resolve a consumer's claim (staff commentary 205.11(c)(4)–5).

If, after investigating the alleged error, the financial institution determines that an error has occurred, it must promptly (within one business day after such determination) correct the error, including the crediting of interest, if applicable. The financial institution must provide within three business days of the completed investigation an oral or written report of the correction to the consumer and, as applicable, notify the consumer that the provisional credit has been made final (section 205.11(c)(2)(iii) and (iv)).

If the financial institution determines that no error occurred or that an error occurred in a different manner or amount from that described by the consumer, the financial institution must mail or deliver a written explanation of its findings within three business days after concluding its investigation. The explanation must include a notice of the consumer's rights to request the documents upon which the financial institution relied in making its determination (section 205.11(d)(1)). Upon request from the consumer, the financial institution must promptly mail or deliver to the consumer copies of documents upon which it relied in making its determination (section 205.11(d)(2)).

Upon debiting a provisionally credited amount, the financial institution must notify the consumer of the date and amount of the debit and of the fact that the financial institution will honor (without charge) checks, drafts, or similar paper instruments payable to third parties and preauthorized debits for five business days after transmittal of the notice. The financial institution need honor only items that it would have paid if the provisionally credited funds had not been debited.

If a notice involves an error that occurred within 30 days after the first deposit to the account was made, the time periods are extended from 10 and 45 days, to 20 and 90 days, respectively. If the notice of error involves a transaction that was not initiated in a state or resulted from a POS debit card transaction, the 45-day period is extended to 90 days (section 205.11(c)(3)).

If a financial institution has fully complied with the investigation requirements, it generally does not need to reinvestigate if a consumer later reasserts the same error. It must investigate, however, a claim of error asserted by a consumer following receipt of information provided pursuant to section 205.11(a)(1)(vii) (section 205.11(e)).

VI. Receipts and Periodic Statements

Documentation of Transfers–Section 205.9

Electronic terminal receipts. Receipts must be made available at the time a consumer initiates an EFT at an electronic terminal (section 205.9(a)). Financial institutions may provide receipts only to consumers who request one (staff commentary 205.9(a)–1). The receipt must include, as applicable:

- **Amount of the transfer.** A charge for making the transfer may be included in the amount, provided the charge is disclosed on the receipt, and on a sign posted on or at the terminal.
- **Date.** The date the consumer initiates the transfer.
- **Type of transfer and type of account.** Descriptions such as "withdrawal from checking" or "transfer from savings to checking" are appropriate. This is true even if the accounts are only similar in function to a checking account (such as a share draft or negotiable order of withdrawal (NOW)

account) or a savings account (such as a share account). If the access device used can only access one account, the type of account may be omitted (staff commentaries 205.9(a)(3)–1; 205.9(3)–2; 205.9(3)–4; and 205.9(3)–5).

- **Number or code identifying the consumer's account(s) or the access device used to initiate the transfer.** The number and code need not exceed four digits or letters.
- **Location of the terminal.** The location of the terminal where the transfer is initiated or an identification, such as a code or terminal number. If the location is disclosed, except in limited circumstances where all terminals are located in the same city or state, the receipt must include the city and state or foreign country and one of the following:
  - Street address of the terminal;
  - Generally accepted name for the location of the terminal (such as an airport, shopping center, or branch of a financial institution); or
  - Name of the entity (if other than the financial institution providing the statement) at whose place of business the terminal is located, such as a store, and the city, state, or foreign country (section 205.9(a)(5)).
- **Name of any third party to or from whom funds are transferred.** A code may be used to identify the party if the code is explained on the receipt. This requirement does not apply if the name of the party is provided by the consumer in a manner the terminal cannot duplicate on the receipt, such as on a payment stub (section 205.9(a)(6) and staff commentary 205.9(a)(6)–1).

Receipts are not required for EFTs of $15 or less (section 205.9(e)).

Periodic statements. Periodic statements must be sent for each monthly cycle in which an EFT has occurred, and at least quarterly if no EFT has occurred (section 205.9(b)). For each EFT made during the cycle, the statement must include, as applicable:

- Amount of the transfer. If a charge was imposed at an electronic terminal by the owner or operator of the terminal, that charge may be included in the amount.
- Date the transfer was posted to the account.
- Type of transfer(s) and type of account(s) to or from which funds were transferred.

- For each transfer (except deposits of cash, or a check, draft, or similar paper instrument to the consumer's account) initiated at an electronic terminal, the terminal location as required for the receipt under section 205.9(a)(5).
- Name of any third-party payee or payor.
- Account number(s).
- Total amount of any fees and charges, other than a finance charge as defined by Regulation Z, assessed during the period for making EFTs, the right to make EFTs, or for account maintenance.
- Balance in the account at the beginning and close of the statement period.
- Address and telephone number to be used by the consumer for inquiries or notice of errors. If the financial institution has elected to send the abbreviated error notice with every periodic statement, the address and telephone number may appear on that document.
- If the financial institution has provided a telephone number which the consumer can use to find out whether or not a preauthorized transfer has taken place, that telephone number.

Exceptions to the Periodic Statement Requirement for Certain Accounts

Passbook accounts. When a consumer's passbook may not be accessed by an EFT other than preauthorized transfers to the account, a periodic statement need not be sent, provided that the financial institution updates the consumer's passbook or provides the required information on a separate document at the consumer's request. To update the passbook, the amount and date of each EFT made since the passbook was last presented must be listed (section 205.9(c)(1)(i)). For other accounts that may be accessed only by preauthorized transfers to the account, the financial institution must send a periodic statement at least quarterly (section 205.9(c)(1)(ii)).

Transfers between accounts. If a transfer occurs between two accounts of the consumer at the same financial institution, the transfer need only be documented for one of the two accounts (section 205.9(c)(2)). A preauthorized transfer between two accounts of the consumer at the same financial institution is subject to the section 205.9(c)(1) rule on preauthorized transfers and not the section 205.9(c)(2) rule on intra-institutional transfers (section 205.9(c)(3)).

Documentation for foreign-initiated transfers. If an EFT is initiated outside the United States, the financial institution need not provide a receipt or a periodic statement reflecting the transfer if it treats an inquiry for clarification or documentation as a notice of error (section 205.9(d)).

Alternatives to Periodic Statements for Financial Institutions Offering Payroll Card Accounts–Section 205.18

This section provides an alternative to providing periodic statements for payroll card accounts if financial institutions make the account information available to consumers by specific means. In addition, this section clarifies how financial institutions that do not provide periodic statements for payroll card accounts can comply with the Regulation E requirements relating to initial disclosures, the annual error resolution notice, liability limits, and the error resolution procedures.

Typically, employers and third-party service providers do not meet the definition of a "financial institution" subject to the regulation because they neither (i) hold payroll card accounts nor (ii) issue payroll cards and agree with consumers to provide EFT services in connection with payroll card accounts. To the extent an employer or a service provider undertakes either of these functions, however, it would be deemed a financial institution under the regulation (staff commentary 205.18(a)–2).

Alternative to periodic statements. A financial institution does not need to furnish periodic statements required by section 205.9(b) if the financial institution makes available to the consumer the following:

- The account balance, through a readily available telephone line.
- An electronic history of account transactions covering at least 60 days preceding the date the consumer electronically accesses the account.
- A written history of the account transactions provided promptly in response to an oral or written request and covering at least 60 days preceding the date the financial institution receives the consumer's request (section 205.18(b)(1)).

The history of account transactions must include the same type of information required on periodic statements under section 205.9(b) (section 205.18(b)(2)).

Requirements to comply with Regulation E. If a financial institution provides an alternative to periodic statements under section 205.18(b), it must comply with the following:

- Modify the initial disclosures under 205.7(b) by disclosing
  - A telephone number that the consumer may call to obtain the account balance; the means by which the consumer can obtain an electronic account history, such as a Web site address; and a summary of the consumer's right to receive a written account history upon request (in place of the summary of the right to receive a periodic statement required by section 205.7(b)(6)), including a telephone number to call to request a history. The disclosure required by section 205.18(c)(1)(i) may be made by providing a notice substantially similar to the notice contained in paragraph A–7(a) in appendix A of part 205.
  - A notice concerning error resolution that is substantially similar to the notice contained in paragraph A–7(b) in appendix A, in place of the notice required by section 205.7(b)(10).
- Provide an annual error resolution notice that is substantially similar to the notice contained in paragraph (b) to A–7—Model Clauses for Financial Institutions Offering Payroll Card Accounts in appendix A of part 205, in place of the notice required by section 205.8(b). Alternatively, a financial institution may include on or with each electronic and written history provided in accordance with section 205.18(b)(1), a notice substantially similar to the abbreviated notice for periodic statements contained in paragraph A–3(b) in appendix A, modified as necessary to reflect the error-resolution provisions set forth in this section.
- Set limits on consumer liability.
  - For purposes of section 205.6(b)(3), the 60-day period for reporting any unauthorized transfer begins on the earlier of
    o the date the consumer electronically accesses the consumer's account under section 205.18(b)(1)(ii), provided that the electronic history made available to the consumer reflects the transfer; or
    o the date the financial institution sends a written history of the consumer's account transactions requested by the consumer under section 205.18(b)(1)(iii) in which the unauthorized transfer is first reflected.
  - A financial institution may limit the consumer's liability for an unauthorized transfer as provided under section 205.6(b)(3) for transfers reported by the consumer within 120 days after the transfer was credited or debited to the consumer's account.

- Comply with error resolution requirements.
  - An error notice is considered timely, and the financial institution must comply with the requirements of section 205.11, if the financial institution receives notice from the consumer no later than the earlier of
    - o 60 days after the date the consumer electronically accesses the consumer's account under section 205.18(b)(1)(ii), provided that the electronic history made available to the consumer reflects the alleged error; or
    - o 60 days after the date the financial institution sends a written history of the consumer's account transactions requested by the consumer under section 205.18(b)(1)(iii) in which the alleged error is first reflected.
  - Alternatively, a financial institution complies with the error resolution requirements in section 205.11 if it investigates any oral or written notice of an error from the consumer that is received by the financial institution within 120 days after the transfer allegedly in error was credited or debited to the consumer's account.

VII. Gift Cards

Background

A gift card is a type of prepaid card that is designed to be purchased by one consumer and given to another consumer as a present or expression of appreciation or recognition. When the gift card is provided in the form of a plastic card, a user of a gift card is able to access and spend the value associated with the device by swiping the card at a POS terminal, much as a person would use a debit card. There are two distinct types of gift cards: closed-loop cards and open-loop cards. Closed-loop gift cards constitute the majority of the gift card market; are typically issued by a merchant, not by a financial institution; and generally can only be used to make purchases at the merchant or group of merchants. Open-loop gift cards are generally issued by financial institutions, typically carry a card network brand logo, can be used at a wide variety of merchants, and are more likely to carry fees compared to closed-loop gift cards, including card issuance and transaction-based fees. Open-loop gift cards are more likely to offer the capability of being reloaded with additional value (reloadable) than are closed-loop gift cards.

Concerns have been raised regarding the amount of fees associated with gift cards, the expiration dates of gift cards, and the adequacy of disclosures. Consumers who do not use the value of the card within a short period of time may be surprised to find that the card has expired or that dormancy or service fees have reduced the value of the card. Even where fees or terms are disclosed on or with the card, the disclosures may not be clear and conspicuous. Section 205.20 contains restrictions on dormancy, inactivity and service fees, and expiration dates.

Scope of the gift card rule (section 205.20(a) and (b)). The rule is generally limited to gift certificates, store gift cards, or general-use prepaid cards sold or issued to consumers primarily for personal, family, or household purposes. It generally does not apply to cards, codes, or other devices that are reloadable and not marketed or labeled as gift cards or gift certificates and loyalty awards; and promotional gift cards. See also the exclusions from the gift card definitions described above.

Restrictions on dormancy, inactivity, or service fees (section 205.20(d)). No person may impose a dormancy, inactivity, or service fee with respect to a gift certificate, store gift card, or general-use prepaid card, unless three conditions are satisfied:

- There has been no activity with respect to the certificate or card within the one-year period before the imposition of the fee,
- Only one such fee is assessed in a given calendar month, and
- Disclosures regarding dormancy, inactivity, or service fees are clearly and conspicuously stated on the certificate or card, and the person issuing or selling the certificate or card has provided these disclosures to the purchaser before the certificate or card is purchased. See the disclosure section, above, for additional information.

Expiration date restrictions (section 205.20(e)). A gift certificate, store gift card, or general-use prepaid card may not be sold or issued unless the expiration date of the funds underlying the certificate or card is no less than five years after the date of issuance (in the case of a gift certificate) or five years after the date of last load of funds (in the case of a store gift card or general-use prepaid card). In addition, information regarding whether funds underlying a certificate or card may expire must be clearly and conspicuously stated on the certificate or card and disclosed before purchase.

No person may sell or issue a certificate or card with an expiration date unless the person has established policies and procedures to provide consumers with a reasonable opportunity to purchase a certificate or card that has an expiration date that is at least five years from the date of purchase. A person who has established policies and procedures to prevent the sale of a certificate or card with less than five years from the date of purchase satisfies this requirement.

A certificate or card generally must include a disclosure alerting consumers to the difference between the certificate or card expiration date and the funds expiration date, if any, and stating that the consumer may contact the issuer for a replacement card. This disclosure must be stated with equal prominence and in close proximity to the certificate or card expiration date. Non-reloadable certificates or cards that bear an expiration date on the certificate or card that is at least seven years from the date of manufacture need not include this disclosure. See the disclosure section, above, for additional information.

To ensure that consumers are able to access the underlying funds for the full five-year period, fees may not be imposed for replacing an expired certificate or card if the underlying funds remain valid (unless the card has been lost or stolen). In lieu of sending a replacement certificate or card, issuers may remit, without charge, the remaining balance of funds to the consumer.

Effective date. The requirements of this section apply to any gift certificate, store gift card, or general-use prepaid card sold to a consumer on or after August 22, 2010, or provided to the consumer as a replacement for such certificate or card.

VIII. Other Requirements

Preauthorized Transfers–Section 205.10

A preauthorized transfer may be either a credit to, or a debit from, an account.

Preauthorized transfers to a consumer's account. When an account is scheduled to be credited by a preauthorized EFT from the same payor at least once every 60 days, the financial institution must provide some form of notice to the consumer so that the consumer can find out whether or not the transfer occurred (section 205.10(a)). The notice requirement will be satisfied if the payor provides notice to the consumer that the transfer has been initiated. If the payor does not provide notice, the financial institution must adopt one of three alternative procedures for giving notice:

- The financial institution may give the consumer oral or written notice within two business days after a preauthorized transfer occurs.
- The financial institution may give the consumer oral or written notice, within two business days after the preauthorized transfer was scheduled to occur, that the transfer did not occur.
- The financial institution may establish a readily available telephone line[13] that the consumer may call to find out whether a preauthorized transfer has occurred. If the financial institution selects this option, the telephone number must be disclosed on the initial disclosures and on each periodic statement.

The financial institution need not use any specific language to give notice but may not simply provide the current account balance (staff commentary 205.10(a)(1)–1). The financial institution may use different methods of notice for different types of preauthorized transfers and need not offer consumers a choice of notice methods (staff commentary 205.10(a)(1)–2).

The financial institution that receives a preauthorized transfer must credit the consumer's account as of the day the funds are received (section 205.10(a)(3)).

Preauthorized transfers from a customer's account. Preauthorized transfers from a consumer's account may be authorized only by the consumer in writing and signed or similarly authenticated by the consumer (section 205.10(b)). Signed, written authorizations may be provided electronically, subject to the E-Sign Act (staff commentary 205.10(b)–5). In all cases, the party that obtains the authorization from the consumer must provide a copy to the consumer. If a third-party payee fails to obtain an authorization in writing or fails to provide a copy to the consumer, the third-party payee, and not the financial institution has violated Regulation E (staff commentary 205.10(b)–2).

---

[13] The telephone line must be "readily available" so that consumers calling to inquire about transfers are able to have their calls answered reasonably promptly during normal business hours. During the initial call in most cases and within two business days after the initial call in all cases, the financial institution should be able to verify whether the transfer was received (staff commentary 205.10(a)(1)–5). Within its primary service area, a financial institution must provide a local or toll-free telephone number (staff commentary 205.10(a)(1)–7).

Stop payments. Consumers have the right to stop payment of preauthorized transfers from accounts. The consumer must notify the financial institution orally or in writing at any time up to three business days before the scheduled date of the transfer (section 205.10(c)(1)). If the debit item is resubmitted, the institution must continue to honor the stop-payment order (staff commentary 205.10(c)(1)). The financial institution may require written confirmation of an oral stop payment order to be made within 14 days of the consumer's oral notification. If the financial institution requires a written confirmation, it must inform the consumer at the time of the oral stop payment order that written confirmation is required and provide the address to which the confirmation should be sent. If the consumer fails to provide written confirmation, the oral stop payment order ceases to be binding after 14 days (section 205.10(c)(2)).

Notice of transfers varying in amount. If a preauthorized transfer from a consumer's account varies in amount from the previous transfer under the same authorization or the preauthorized amount, either the financial institution or the designated payee must send to the consumer a written notice, at least 10 days before the scheduled transfer date, of the amount and scheduled date of the transfer (section 205.10(d)(1)). The consumer may elect to receive notice only when the amount varies by more than an agreed amount or falls outside a specified range (section 205.10(d)(2)). The range must be an acceptable range that the consumer could reasonably anticipate (staff commentary 205.10(d)(2)–1). The financial institution does not violate Regulation E if the payee fails to provide sufficient notice (staff commentary 205.10(d)–1).

Compulsory use. The financial institution may not make it a condition for an extension of credit that repayment will be by means of preauthorized EFT, except for credit extended under an overdraft credit plan or extended to maintain a specified minimum balance in the consumer's account (section 205.10(e)(1)). The financial institution may offer a reduced annual percentage rate (APR) or other cost-related incentive for an automatic payment feature as long as the creditor offers other loan programs for the type of credit involved (staff commentary 205.10(e)(1)–1).[14]

---

[14] This section also prohibits anyone from requiring the establishment of an account for receipt of EFTs with a particular financial institution either as a condition of employment or the receipt of a government benefit (section 205.10(e)(2)). The employer may, however, require direct deposit of salary, as long as the employee may choose the financial institution that will accept the direct deposit, or limit direct deposits to one financial institution, as long as the employee may choose to receive salary by other means (e.g., check or cash) (staff commentary 205.10(e)(2)–1).

Services Offered by Provider Not Holding Consumer's Account–Section 205.14

A person who provides EFT services to a consumer but does not hold the consumer's account is a service provider subject to section 205.14 if the person issues an access device that the consumer can use to access the account and no agreement exists between the person and the account-holding financial institution. Transfers initiated by a service provider are often cleared through an ACH.

The responsibilities of the service provider are set forth in sections 205.14(b)(1) and (2). The duties of the account-holding financial institution with respect to the service provider are found in sections 205.14(c)(l) and (2).

Electronic Fund Transfer of Government Benefits–Section 205.15

Section 205.15 contains the rules that apply to electronic benefit transfer programs. It provides that government agencies must comply with modified rules on the issuance of access devices, periodic statements, initial disclosures, liability for unauthorized use, and error resolution notices.

IX. Relation to Other Laws

This section describes the relationship between the EFTA and the Truth in Lending Act. The section also provides procedures for states to apply for exemptions from the requirements of the EFTA or Regulation E for any class of EFTs within the state.

The EFTA governs the following:

- The issuance of debit cards and other access devices with EFT capabilities.
- The addition of EFT features to credit cards.
- The issuance of access devices whose only credit feature is a pre-existing agreement to extend credit to cover account overdrafts or to maintain a minimum account balance, or is an overdraft service.

The Truth in Lending Act governs all of the following:

- The issuance of credit cards as defined in Regulation Z.
- The addition of a credit feature to a debit card or other access device, other than an overdraft service.

- The issuance of dual debit/credit cards, except for access devices whose only credit feature is a pre-existing agreement to cover account overdrafts or to maintain a minimum account balance, or is an overdraft service.

The EFTA and Regulation E preempt inconsistent state laws but only to the extent of the inconsistency. The Board is given the authority to determine whether a state law is inconsistent. A financial institution, state, or other interested party may request the Board to make such a determination. A state law will not be deemed inconsistent if it is more protective of the consumer than the EFTA or Regulation E. Upon application, the Board has the authority to exempt any state from the requirements of the act or the regulation for any class of EFTs within a state, with the exception of the civil liability provision.

X.   Administrative Enforcement and Record Retention

Section 917 of the EFTA sets forth the federal agencies responsible for enforcing compliance with the provisions of the act.

Record retention. Financial institutions must maintain evidence of compliance with the EFTA and Regulation E for at least two years. The agency supervising the financial institution may extend this period. The period may also be extended if the financial institution is subject to an action filed under sections 910, 915 or 916(a) of the EFTA, which generally apply to the financial institution's liability under the EFTA and Regulation E. Persons subject to the EFTA who have actual notice that they are being investigated or subject to an enforcement proceeding must retain records until disposition of the proceeding.

Records may be stored on microfiche, microfilm, magnetic tape, or in any other manner capable of accurately retaining and reproducing the information.

XI.   Miscellaneous

EFTA contains several additional provisions that are not directly reflected in the language of Regulation E. Most significantly, 15 USC 1693l provides that the consumer may not waive by agreement any right conferred, or cause of action created, by the EFTA. The consumer and another person, however, may provide by agreement greater consumer protections or additional rights or remedies than those provided by EFTA. In addition, the consumer may sign a waiver in settlement of a dispute.

If a third party payee has agreed to accept payment by EFT, the consumer's obligation to pay is suspended during any period in which a system malfunction prevents an EFT from occurring (15 USC 1693j). The payee, however, may avoid that suspension by making a written request for payment by means other than EFT.

Failure to comply with the requirements of EFTA can result in civil and criminal liability, as outlined in 15 USC 1693m and 15 USC 1693n. Financial institutions may also be liable for damages under 15 USC 1693h because of failure to complete an EFT or failure to stop a preauthorized transfer when instructed to do so.

Model disclosure clauses and forms (12 CFR 205, appendix A). Appendix A of Regulation E contains model clauses and forms that financial institutions may use to comply with the requirement disclosure requirements of Regulation E. Use of the model forms is optional and a financial institution may make certain changes to the language or format of the model forms without losing the protection from civil and criminal liability under sections 915 and 916 of the EFTA. The model forms are:

A–1 **Model Clauses for Unsolicited Issuance** (Section 205.5(b)(2))

A–2 **Model Clauses for Initial Disclosures** (Section 205.7(b))

A–3 **Model Forms for Error Resolution Notice** (Section 205.7(b)(10) and 205.8(b))

A–4 **Model Form for Service-Providing Institutions** (Section 205.14(b)(1)(ii))

A–5 **Model Forms for Government Agencies** (Section 205.15(d)(1) and(2))

A–6 **Model Clauses for Authorizing One-Time Electronic Fund Transfers Using Information from a Check** (Section 205.3(b)(2))

A–7 **Model Clauses for Financial Institutions Offering Payroll Card Accounts** (Section 205.18(c))

A–8 **Model Clause for Electronic Collection of Returned Item Fees** (Section 205.3(b)(3))

A–9 **Model Consent Form for Overdraft Services** (Section 205.17)

Electronic Fund Transfer Act— Regulation E

Expanded Procedures

Objective

Determine the bank's level of compliance with the Truth in Lending Act and Regulation E.

Assess the bank's level of compliance by using the EFTA Worksheet.

EFTA Worksheet

Use this worksheet for reviewing audit work papers, evaluating bank policies, performing transaction testing, and training, as appropriate. Complete only those aspects of the worksheet that specifically relate to the issue being reviewed, evaluated, or tested and retain those completed sections in the work papers.

When reviewing audits or evaluating bank policies, a "no" answer indicates a possible exception/deficiency and should be explained in the work papers. When performing transaction testing, a "no" answer indicates a possible violation and should be explained in the work papers. If a line item is not applicable within the area you are reviewing, just indicate "NA."

Underline the applicable use: Audit   Bank Policies   Transaction Testing

EFTA Worksheet	Yes	No	NA
12 CFR 205.5–Issuance of Access Devices			
1. Do the financial institution's policies, practices, and procedures allow that validated access devices are issued only			
• in response to oral or written requests (12 CFR 205.5(a)(1)) or			
• as a renewal or substitution for an accepted access device? (12 CFR 205.5(a)(2))			
2. Do the financial institution's policies, practices, and procedures allow that unsolicited access devices are issued only when the devices are			
• not validated? (12 CFR 205.5(b)(1))			
• accompanied by a clear explanation that they are not validated and how they may be disposed of if validation is not desired? (12 CFR 205.5(b)(2))			
• accompanied by the initial disclosures required by 12 CFR 205.7? (12 CFR 205.5(b)(3))			
• validated only in response to a consumer's request and after the financial institution has verified the consumer's identity by reasonable means (e.g., photograph, fingerprint, personal visit, and signature)? (12 CFR 205.5(b)(4) and staff commentary)			

EFTA Worksheet	Yes	No	NA
12 CFR 205.6–Consumer Liability for Unauthorized Electronic Fund Transfers			
3. Does the financial institution impose liability on the consumer for unauthorized transfers only if (12 CFR 205.6(a))			
• any access device that was used was an accepted access device?			
• the institution has provided a means to identify the consumer to whom it was issued?			
• the institution has provided the disclosures required by section 205.7(b)(l), (2), and (3)?			
4. Does the financial institution NOT rely on consumer negligence or the deposit agreement to impose greater consumer liability for unauthorized EFTs than is permitted under Regulation E? (staff commentaries 205.6(b)–1 and –2)			
5. If a consumer notifies the financial institution within two business days after learning of the loss or theft of an access device, does the financial institution limit the consumer's liability for unauthorized EFTs to the lesser of $50 or actual loss? (12 CFR 205.6(b)(1))			
6. If a consumer does not notify the financial institution within two business days after learning of the loss or theft of an access device, does the institution limit the consumer's liability for unauthorized EFTs to the lesser of $500 or the sum of (12 CFR 205.6(b)(2))			
• $50 or the amount of unauthorized EFTs that occurred within the two business days, whichever is less; and (12 CFR205.6(b)(2)(i))			
• the dollar amount from unauthorized EFTs that occurred after the close of two business days and before notice to the financial institution (provided the financial institution establishes that these transfers would not have occurred had the consumer notified the financial institution within that two-day period)? (12 CFR205.6(b)(2)(ii))			
7. If a consumer notifies the financial institution of an unauthorized EFT within 60 calendar days of transmittal of the periodic statement upon which the unauthorized EFT appears, does the financial institution not hold the consumer liable for the subsequent unauthorized transfers that occur? (12 CFR 205.6(b)(3))			

EFTA Worksheet	Yes	No	NA
8. If a consumer does not notify the financial institution of an unauthorized EFT within 60 calendar days of transmittal of the periodic statement upon which the unauthorized EFT appears, does the financial institution ensure that the consumer's liability does not exceed the amount of the unauthorized transfers that occur after the close of the 60 days and before notice to the financial institution, if the financial institution establishes that the transfers would not have occurred had timely notice been given? (12 CFR 205.6(b)(3))			
9. If a consumer notifies the financial institution of an unauthorized EFT within the time frames discussed in questions 7 or 8 and the consumer's access device is involved in the unauthorized transfer, does the financial institution hold the consumer liable for amounts as set forth in 12 CFR 205.6(b)(1) or (2) (discussed in questions 5 and 6)? (12 CFR 205.6(b)(3)) Note: The first two tiers of liability (as set forth in 12 CFR 205.6(b)(1) and (2) and discussed in questions 5 and 6) do not apply to unauthorized transfers from a consumer's account made without an access device. (staff commentary 205.6(b)(3)–2)			
10. Does the financial institution extend the 60-day time period by a reasonable amount, if the consumer's delay in notification was due to extenuating circumstance? (12 CFR 205.6(b)(4))			
11. Does the financial institution consider notice to be made when the consumer takes steps reasonably necessary to provide the institution with pertinent information, whether or not a particular employee or agent of the institution actually received the information? (12 CFR 205.6(b)(5)(i))			
12. Does the financial institution allow the consumer to provide notice in person, by telephone, or in writing? (12 CFR 205.6(b)(5)(ii))			
13. Does the financial institution considers written notice to be given at the time the consumer mails or delivers the notice for transmission to the institution by any other usual means? (12 CFR 205.6(b)(5)(iii))			
14. Does the financial institution consider notice given when it becomes aware of circumstances leading to the reasonable belief that an unauthorized transfer to or from the consumer's account has been or may be made? (12 CFR 205.6(b)(5)(iii))			
15. Does the financial institution limit the consumer's liability to a lesser amount than provided by 12 CFR 205.6 when state law or an agreement between the consumer and the financial institution provide for such an amount? (12 CFR 205.6(b)(6))			

EFTA Worksheet	Yes	No	NA
12 CFR 205.7–Initial Disclosures			
16.	Does the financial institution provide the initial disclosures at the time a consumer contracts for an EFT service or before the first EFT is made involving the consumer's account? (12 CFR 205.7(a))			
17.	Do the financial institution's initial disclosures provide the following information, as applicable:			
	• A summary of the consumer's liability for unauthorized transfers under 12 CFR 205.6 or under state or other applicable law or agreement? (12 CFR 205.7(b)(1))			
	• The telephone number and address of the person or office to be notified when the consumer believes that an unauthorized EFT has been or may be made? (12 CFR 205.7(b)(2))			
	• The financial institution's business days? (12 CFR 205.7(b)(3))			
	• The type of EFTs the consumer may make and any limits on the frequency and dollar amount of transfers? (If details on the limits on frequency and dollar amount are essential to maintain the security of the system, they need not be disclosed.) (12 CFR 205.7(b)(4))			
	• Any fees imposed by the financial institution for EFTs or for the right to make transfers? (12 CFR 205.7(b)(5))			
	• A summary of the consumer's right to receive receipts and periodic statements, as provided in 12 CFR 205.9, and notices regarding preauthorized transfers as provided in 12 CFR 205.10(a) and 205.10(d)? (12 CFR 205.7(b)(6))			
	• A summary of the consumer's right to stop payment of a preauthorized EFT and the procedure for placing a stop payment order, as provided in 12 CFR 205.10(c)? (12 CFR 205.7(b)(7))			
	• A summary of the financial institution's liability to the consumer for its failure to make or to stop certain transfers under the EFTA? (12 CFR 205.7(b)(8))			
	• The circumstances under which the financial institution, in the ordinary course of business, may disclose information to third parties concerning the consumer's account? (12 CFR 205.7(b)(9))			
	• An error resolution notice that is substantially similar to the Model Form A–3 in appendix A? (12 CFR 205.7(b)(10))			

EFTA Worksheet	Yes	No	NA
• A notice that a fee may be imposed by an ATM operator (as defined in section 205.16(a)) when the consumer initiates an EFT or makes a balance inquiry and by any network used to complete the transaction? (12 CFR 205.7(b)(11))			
18. Does the financial institution provide disclosures at the time a new EFT service is added, if the terms and conditions of the service are different from those initially disclosed? (12 CFR 205.7(c))			
12 CFR 205.8–Change-in-Terms Notice; Error Resolution Notice			
19. If the financial institution made any changes in terms or conditions required to be disclosed under section 205.7(b) that would result in increased fees, increased liability, fewer types of available EFTs, or stricter limits on the frequency or dollar amount of transfers, did the financial institution provide a written notice to consumers at least 21 days before the effective date of such change? (12 CFR 205.8(a)(1))			
20. Does the financial institution provide either the long form error resolution notice at least once every calendar year or the short form error resolution notice on each periodic statement? (12 CFR 205.8(b))			
12 CFR 205.9–Receipts at Electronic Terminals; Periodic Statements			
21. Does the financial institution make receipts available to the consumer at the time the consumer initiates an EFT at an electronic terminal? The financial institution is exempt from this requirement for EFTs of $15 or less. (12 CFR 205.9(a) and (e))			
22. Do the receipts contain the following information, as applicable:			
• The amount of the transfer? (12 CFR 205.9(a)(1))			
• The date the transfer was initiated? (12 CFR 205.9(a)(2))			
• The type of transfer and the type of account to or from which funds were transferred? (12 CFR 205.9(a)(3))			
• A number or code that identifies the consumer's account or the access device used to initiate the transfer? (12 CFR 205.9(a)(4))			
• The terminal location where the transfer is initiated? (12 CFR 205.9(a)(5))			
• The name or other identifying information of any third party to or from whom funds are transferred? (12 CFR 205.9(a)(6))			

EFTA Worksheet	Yes	No	NA
23. Does the financial institution send a periodic statement for each monthly cycle in which an EFT has occurred? If no EFT occurred, does the financial institution send a periodic statement at least quarterly? (12 CFR 205.9(b))			
24. Does the periodic statement contain the following information, as applicable:			
• Transaction information for each EFT occurring during the cycle, including the			
– Amount of transfer; (12 CFR 205.9(b)(1)(i))			
– Date of transfer, (12 CFR 205.9(b)(1)(iI))			
– Type of transfer, (12 CFR 205.9(b)(1)(iii))			
– Terminal location, and (12 CFR 205.9(b)(1)(iv))			
– Name of any third party transferor or transferee? (12 CFR 205.9(b)(1)(v))			
• Account number? (12 CFR 205.9(b)(2))			
• Fees? (12 CFR 205.9(b)(3))			
• Account balances? (12 CFR 205.9(b)(4))			
• Address and telephone number for inquiries? (12 CFR 205.9(b)(5))			
• Telephone number to ascertain preauthorized transfers, if the financial institution provides telephone notice under 12 CFR 205.10(a)(1)(iii)? (12 CFR 205.9(b)(6))			
12 CFR 205.10–Preauthorized Transfers			
25. If a consumer's account is to be credited by a preauthorized EFT from the same payor at least once every 60 days (and the payor does not already provide notice to the consumer that the transfer has been initiated) (12 CFR 205.10(a)(2)), does the financial institution do one of the following:			
• Provide oral or written notice, within two business days, after the transfer occurs? (12 CFR 205.10(a)(1)(i))			
• Provide oral or written notice, within two business days after the transfer was scheduled to occur, that the transfer did or did not occur? (12 CFR 205.10(a)(1)(ii))			

EFTA Worksheet	Yes	No	NA
• Provide a readily available telephone line that the consumer can call to determine if the transfer occurred and that telephone number is disclosed on the initial disclosure of account terms and on each periodic statement? (12 CFR 205.10(a)(1)(iii))			
26. Does the financial institution credit the amount of a preauthorized transfer as of the date the funds for the transfer are received? (12 CFR 205.10(a)(3))			
27. Does the financial institution ensure that an authorization is obtained for preauthorized transfers from a consumer's account by a written, signed, or similarly authenticated authorization and is a copy of the authorization provided to the consumer? (12 CFR 205.10(b))			
28. Does the financial institution allow the consumer to stop payment on a preauthorized EFT by oral or written notice at least three business days before the scheduled date of the transfer? (12 CFR 205.10(c)(1))			
29. If the financial institution requires that the consumer give written confirmation of an oral stop-payment order within 14 days, does the financial institution inform the consumer, at the time the consumer gives oral notification, of the requirement and provide the address where the consumer must send the written confirmation? (12 CFR 205.10(c)(2)) Note: An oral stop-payment order ceases to be binding after 14 days if the consumer fails to provide the required written confirmation.			
30. Does the financial institution inform, or ensure that third-party payees inform, the consumer of the right to receive notice of all varying transfers?			
OR			
Does the financial institution give the consumer the option of receiving notice only when a transfer falls outside a specified range of amounts or differs from the most recent transfer by an agreed-upon amount? (12 CFR 205.10(d)(2))			
31. If the financial institution or third-party payee is obligated to send the consumer written notice of the EFT of a varying amount, does the financial institution ensure that			
• the notice contains the amount and date of transfer? (12 CFR 205.10(d)(1))			
• the notice is sent at least 10 days before the scheduled date of transfer? (12 CFR 205.10(d)(1))			

EFTA Worksheet	Yes	No	NA
32. Does the financial institution not condition an extension of credit to a consumer on the repayment of loans by preauthorized EFT, except for credit extended under an overdraft credit plan or extended to maintain a specified minimum balance in the consumer's account? (12 CFR 205.10(e)(1))			
33. Does the financial institution not require a consumer to establish an account for EFTs with a particular institution as a condition of employment or receipt of government benefits? (12 CFR 205.10(e)(2))			
12 CFR 205.11–Procedures for Resolving Errors			
34. Does the financial institution have procedures to investigate and resolve all oral or written notices of error received no later than 60 days after the institution sends the periodic statement or provides passbook documentation? (12 CFR 205.11(b)(1)(i))			
35. If the financial institution requires written confirmation of an error within 10 business days of an oral notice, does the financial institution inform the consumer of this requirement and provide the address where the written confirmation must be sent? (12 CFR 205.11(b)(2))			
36. Does the financial institution have procedures to investigate and resolve alleged errors within 10 business days, except as otherwise provided in 12 CFR 205.11(c)? (12 CFR 205.11(c)(1))			
37. Does the financial institution report investigation results to the consumer within three business days after completing its investigation and correct any error within one business day after determining that an error occurred? (12 CFR 205.11(c)(1))			
38. If the financial institution is unable to complete its investigation within 10 business days, does the financial institution have procedures to investigate and resolve alleged errors within 45 calendar days of receipt of a notice of error; and			
• Does the financial institution provisionally credit the consumer's account in the amount of the alleged error (including interest, if applicable) within 10 business days of receiving the error notice (however, if the financial institution requires, but does not receive, written confirmation within 10 business days, the financial institution is not required to provisionally credit the consumer's account)? (12 CFR 205.11(c)(2)(i))			

EFTA Worksheet	Yes	No	NA
• Within two business days after granting any provisional credit, does the financial institution inform the consumer of the amount and date of the provisional credit and gives the consumer full use of the funds during the investigation? (12 CFR 205.11(c)(2)(ii))			
• Within one business day after determining that an error occurred, does the financial institution correct the error? and (12 CFR 205.11(c)(2)(iii))			
• Does the financial institution report the results to the consumer within three business days after completing its investigation including, if applicable, notice that a provisional credit has been made final? (12 CFR 205.11(c)(2)(iv))			
39. If a billing error occurred, does the financial institution not impose a charge related to any aspect of the error-resolution process? (staff commentary 205.11(c)–3)			
40. If the financial institution determines that no error occurred (or that an error occurred in a manner or amount different from that described by the consumer), does the financial institution send a written explanation of its findings to the consumer and note the consumer's right to request the documents the financial institution used in making its determination? (12 CFR 205.11(d)(1))			
41. When the financial institution determines that no error (or a different error) occurred, does the financial institution notify the consumer of the date and amount of the debiting of the provisionally credited amount and the fact that the financial institution will continue to honor checks and drafts to third parties and preauthorized transfers for five business days (to the extent that they would have been paid if the provisionally credited funds had not been debited)? (12 CFR 205.11(d)(2))			
12 CFR 205.13–Record Retention			
42. Does the financial institution maintain evidence of compliance with the requirements of the EFTA and Regulation E for a period of two years? (12 CFR 205.13(b))			
12 CFR 205.16–Disclosures at ATMs			
43. If the financial institution operates an ATM and imposes a fee on a consumer for initiating an EFT or balance inquiry, does the financial institution			
• provide notice that a fee will be imposed; and (12 CFR 205.16(b)(1))			
• disclose the amount of the fee? (12 CFR 205.16(b)(2))			

EFTA Worksheet	Yes	No	NA
44. Does the financial institution post the notice required by section 205.16(b) in a prominent and conspicuous location on or at the ATM? (12 CFR 205.16(c)(1))			
45. Does the financial institution provide the notice required by section 205.16(b) either by showing it on the ATM screen or by providing it on paper before the consumer is committed to paying a fee? (12 CFR 205.16(c)(2))			
CFR 205.17–Requirements for Overdraft Services			
46. Does the financial institution's overdraft protection program incorporate the agency's guidance as applicable?			
47. Does the financial institution's overdraft protection program provide "overdraft services," i.e., charge fees for paying ATM and one-time debit overdrafts? (12 CFR 205.17(a)) If no, do not complete this section.			
48. If the financial institution assesses a fee or charge (note: fees or charges may generally be assessed only on transactions paid after the confirmation has been mailed or delivered) on the consumer's account for paying an ATM or one-time debit card transaction pursuant to the financial institutions overdraft service, does the financial institution first (12 CFR 205.17(b)(1)):			
• provide the consumer with a notice in writing, or if the consumer agrees, electronically, that is segregated from all other information and describes the institution's overdraft service (12 CFR 205.17(b)(1)(i));			
• provide a reasonable opportunity for the consumer to affirmatively consent, or opt in, to the institution's payment of ATM and one-time debit card transactions (12 CFR 205.17(b)(1)(ii));			
• obtain the consumer's affirmative consent, or opt in, to the institution's payment of ATM or one-time debit card transactions (12 CFR 205.17(b)(1)(iii)); and			
• provide the consumer with confirmation of the consumer's consent in writing, or, if the consumer agrees, electronically, which includes a statement informing the consumer of the right to revoke such consent? (12 CFR 205.17(b)(1)(iv))			
49. Does the financial institution ensure that it does not condition the payment of any overdrafts for checks, ACH transactions, and other types of transactions on the consumer affirmatively consenting to the institution's payment of ATM and one-time debit card transactions pursuant to the institution's "overdraft services"? (12 CFR 205.17(b)(2)(i))			

EFTA Worksheet	Yes	No	NA
50. Does the financial institution honor paychecks, ACH transactions, and other types of transactions that overdraw the consumer's account regardless of whether the consumer has affirmatively consented to the institution's overdraft protection service for ATM and one-time debit card transactions? (12 CFR 205.17(b)(2)(ii))			
51. For consumers who have **not** opted in, and if an overdraft fee or charge is based on the amount of the outstanding negative balance, does the institution only assess fees where the negative balance is attributable in whole or in part to a check, ACH, or other type of transaction not subject to the prohibition on assessment of overdraft fees? For consumers who have **not** opted in, does the financial institution only assess daily or sustained overdraft, negative balance, or similar fees or charges where the negative balance is attributable in whole or in part to a check, ACH, or other type of transaction not subject to the prohibition on assessment of overdraft fees? Does the institution base the date on which such a daily or sustained overdraft, negative balance, or similar fee or charge is assessed on the date on which the check, ACH, or other type of transaction was paid into overdraft? (staff commentary 205.17(b)–9)			
52. Does the financial institution provide consumers who do not affirmatively consent to the institution's overdraft service for ATM and one-time debit card transactions the same account terms, conditions, and features that it provides to consumers who affirmatively consent, except for the overdraft service for ATM and one-time debit card transactions? (12 CFR 205.17(b)(3))			
53. Is the notice required by12 CFR 205.17(b)(1)(i) substantially similar to Model Form A–9 set forth in appendix A of 12 CFR 205.17, including applicable items from the list below, and does it not contain any additional information? (12 CFR 205.17(d)):			
• Overdraft service: Does the notice provide a brief description of the overdraft service and the types of transactions for which a fee or charge-off paying an overdraft may be imposed, including ATM and one-time debit card transactions? (12 CFR 205.17(d)(1))			

EFTA Worksheet	Yes	No	NA
• Fees imposed: Does the notice contain the dollar amount of any fees or charges assessed by the financial institution for paying an ATM or one-time debit card transaction pursuant to the financial institution's overdraft service, including any daily or other overdraft fees? Note: If the amount of the fee is determined on the basis of the number of times the consumer has overdrawn the account, the amount of the overdraft, or other factors, the institution must disclose the maximum fee that may be imposed. (12 CFR 205.17(d)(2));			
• Limits on fees charged: Does the notice disclose the maximum number of overdraft fees or charges that may be assessed per day, or, if applicable, that there is no limit? (12 CFR 205.17(d)(3))			
• Disclosure of opt-in right: Does the notice explain the consumer's right to affirmatively consent to the financial institution's payment of overdrafts for ATM and one-time debit card transactions pursuant to the institution's overdraft service, including the methods by which the consumer may consent to the service? (12 CFR 205.17(d)(4))			
• Alternative plans for covering overdrafts: As applicable, does the institution's opt-in notice appropriately addresses the alternative methods for covering overdrafts? (12 CFR 205.17(d)(5))			
– If the institution offers both a line of credit subject to the Board's Regulation Z (12 CFR part 226) and a service that transfers funds from another account of the consumer held at the institution to cover overdrafts, does the notice state that both alternative plans are offered? (12 CFR 205.17(d)(5))			
– If the institution offers one, but not the other, does the notice state which of the alternative plans it offers? If the institution does not offer either a line of credit subject to the Board's Regulation Z (12 CFR part 226) or a service that transfers funds from another account of the consumer held at the institution to cover overdrafts plan, does the notice exclude information regarding both of these plans? (12 CFR 205.17(d)(5))			
– If the financial institution offers additional alternatives for paying overdrafts, at its option the institution may (but is not required to) disclose those alternatives. Does its notice describe those alternatives? (12 CFR 205.17(d)(5))			

EFTA Worksheet	Yes	No	NA
• Permitted modifications and additional content: If the institution modifies the notice, are the modifications permitted to indicate that the consumer has the right to opt into, or out of, the payment of overdrafts under the institution's overdraft service for other types of transactions, such as checks, ACH transactions, or automatic bill payments; to provide a means for the consumer to exercise this choice; and to disclose the associated returned item fee and that additional merchant fees may apply? Note: The institution may also disclose the consumer's right to revoke consent. The response portion of Model Form A–9 may be tailored to the methods offered for opting in and may include reasonable methods to identify the account, such as a bar code. For notices provided to consumers who have opened accounts before July 1, 2010, the financial institution may describe the institution's overdraft service with respect to ATM and one-time debit card transactions with a statement such as "After August 15, 2010, we will not authorize and pay overdrafts for the following types of transactions unless you ask us to (see below)." (12 CFR 205.17(d)(6) and staff commentary 20517(d)–1 through –5))			
54. Joint accounts: When two or more consumers jointly hold an account, does the financial institution treat the affirmative consent of any of the joint consumers as affirmative consent for that account and treat the revocation of affirmative consent by any of the joint consumers as revocation of consent for that account? (12 CFR 205.17(e))			
55. Continuing right to opt in or to revoke opt-in: Does the financial institution allow the consumer to affirmatively consent to the financial institution's overdraft service at any time in the manner described in the notice required (12 CFR 205.17(b)(1)(i)) and allow a consumer to revoke consent at any time in the manner made available to the consumer for providing consent? (12 CFR 205.17(f))			
56. Does the financial institution implement a consumer's revocation of consent as soon as reasonably practicable? (12 CFR 205.17(f))			
57. Is the consumer's affirmative consent to the overdraft service effective until revoked by the consumer, or unless the financial institution terminates the service? (12 CFR 205.17(g))			
12 CFR 205.18–Payroll Card Accounts			
58. If the financial institution offers payroll card accounts, does the financial institution EITHER provide periodic statements as required by 12 CFR 205.9(b) OR make available to the consumer			

EFTA Worksheet	Yes	No	NA
• the account balance, through a readily available telephone line, and (12 CFR 205.18(b)(1)(i))			
• an electronic history of the consumer's account transactions, such as through a Web site, that covers at least 60 days preceding the date the consumer electronically accesses the account, and (12 CFR 205.18(b)(1)(ii))			
• a written history of the consumer's account transactions that is provided promptly in response to an oral or written request and that covers at least 60 days preceding the date the financial institution receives the consumer's request? (12 CFR 205.18(b)(1)(iii)) Note: The history of account transactions must include the information set forth in section 205.9(b).			
59. Does the financial institution provide initial disclosures that include, at a minimum			
• a telephone number that the consumer may call to obtain the account balance, the means by which the consumer can obtain an electronic account history, such as a Web site address, and a summary of the consumer's right to receive a written account history upon request, including a telephone number to call to request a history, and (12 CFR 205.18(c)(1)(i))			
• a notice concerning error resolution? (12 CFR 205.18(c)(1)(ii))			
60. Does the financial institution provide an annual notice concerning error resolution or, alternatively, an abbreviated notice with each electronic and written history? (12 CFR 205.18(c)(2))			
61. Does the financial institution begin the 60-day period for reporting any unauthorized transfer under 12 CFR 205.6(b)(3) on the earlier of the date the consumer electronically accesses the consumer's account after the electronic history made available to the consumer reflects the transfer or the date the financial institution sends a written history of the consumer's account transactions requested by the consumer in which the unauthorized transfer is first reflected? (12 CFR 205.18(c)(3)) Note: A financial institution may comply with the provision above by limiting the consumer's liability for an unauthorized transfer as provided under 12 CFR 205.6(b)(3) for any transfer reported by the consumer within 120 days after the transfer was credited or debited to the consumer's account.			

EFTA Worksheet	Yes	No	NA
62. Does the financial institution comply with the error resolution requirements in response to an oral or written notice of an error from the consumer that is received by the earlier of 60 days after the date the consumer electronically accesses the consumer's account after the electronic history made available to the consumer reflects the alleged error or 60 days after the date the financial institution sends a written history of the consumer's account transactions requested by the consumer in which the alleged error is first reflected? (12 CFR 205.18(c)(4)) Note: The financial institution may comply with the requirements for resolving errors by investigating any oral or written notice of an error from the consumer that is received by the institution within 120 days after the transfer allegedly in error was credited or debited to the consumer's account.			
12 CFR 205.20–Requirements for Gift Cards and Gift Certificates			
63. Is the financial institution a party in a certificate or card distribution chain, including but not limited to a card issuer, a program manager, and a retailer of prepaid cards, to the extent it engages in any of the acts covered by that section with respect to gift certificates, store value cards, or general-use prepaid cards, or to loyalty, award, or promotional gift cards? If no, do not complete this section.			
64. Determine if the institution offers consumers, primarily for personal, family, or household purposes, in a specified amount, a card, code, or other device on a prepaid basis, the following:			
• Gift certificates, which may not be increased or reloaded in exchange for payment and are redeemable upon presentation at a single merchant or an affiliated group of merchants for goods and services . (12 CFR 205.20(a)(1))			
• Store gift cards, which may be increased or reloaded, in exchange for payment; and are redeemable upon presentation at a single merchant or an affiliated group of merchants for goods and services. (12 CFR 205.20(a)(2))			
• General-use prepaid cards, which may be increased or reloaded, in exchange for payment; and are redeemable upon presentation at multiple, unaffiliated merchants for goods or services or useable at ATMs. (12 CFR 205.20(a)(3))			
65. Do loyalty, award or promotional gift cards as defined by (12 CFR 205.20(a)(4)), contain the following disclosures as applicable:			

EFTA Worksheet	Yes	No	NA
• A statement indicating that the card, code, or other device is issued for loyalty, award, or promotional purposes, which must be included on the front of the card, code, or other device? (12 CFR 205.20(a)(4)(iii)(A))			
• The expiration date for the underlying funds, which must be included on the front of the card, code, or other device? (12 CFR 205.20(a)(4)(iii)(B))			
• The amount of fees that may be imposed in connection with the card, code, or other device, and the conditions under which they may be imposed, which must be provided with the card, code, or other device? (12 CFR 205.20(a)(4)(iii)(C))			
• A toll-free telephone number and, if one is maintained, a Web site, that a consumer may use to obtain fee information, which must be included on or with the card, code, or other device? (12 CFR 205.20(a)(4)(iii)(D))			
66. If the terms of the gift certificate, store gift card, or general-use prepaid card impose a dormancy, inactivity, or service fee as defined under 12 CFR 205.20(a)(5):			
• Does the financial institution decline to impose any dormancy, inactivity, or service fee if there has been activity with respect to the certificate or card? (12 CFR 205.20(d)(1))			
• As applicable, are the following clearly and conspicuously stated on the gift certificate, store gift card, or general-use prepaid card:			
– The amount of any dormancy, inactivity, or service fee that may be charged; (12 CFR 205.20(d)(2)(i)			
– How often such a fee may be assessed; and (12 CFR 205.20(d)(2)(ii)			
– That such fee may be assessed for inactivity? (12 CFR 205.20(d)(2)(iii))			
• Is the dormancy, inactivity, or service fee imposed limited to one in any given calendar month? (12 CFR 205.20(d)(3))			
67. If the financial institution sells or issues a gift certificate, store gift card, or general-use prepaid card with an expiration date:			
• Has the financial institution established policies and procedures to provide consumers with a reasonable opportunity to purchase a certificate or card with at least five years remaining until the certificate or card expiration date? (12 CFR 205.20(e)(1))			

EFTA Worksheet	Yes	No	NA
• Is the expiration date for the underlying funds at least the latest of five years after the date the gift certificate was initially issued, five years after the date on which funds were last loaded to a store gift card or general-use prepaid card, or the certificate or card expiration date, if any? (12 CFR 205.20(e)(2))			
68. If the financial institution sells or issues a gift certificate, store gift card, or general-use prepaid card with an expiration date, then the following disclosures are provided on the certificate or card, as applicable:			
• The expiration date for the underlying funds, or if the underlying funds do not expire, that fact; (12 CFR 205.20(e)(3)(i))			
• A toll-free number and, if one is maintained, a Web site that a consumer may use to obtain a replacement certificate or card after the certificate or card expires if the underlying funds may be available; and (12 CFR 205.20(e)(3)(ii))			
• Except where a non-reloadable certificate or card bears an expiration date that is at least seven years from the date of manufacture, a statement, disclosed with equal prominence and in close proximity to the certificate or card expiration date, that			
– the certificate or card expires, but the underlying funds either do not expire or expire later than the certificate or card; (12 CFR 205.20(e)(3)(iii)(A))			
– the consumer may contact the issuer for a replacement card; and (12 CFR 205.20(e)(3)(iii)(B))			
– no fee or charge is imposed on the cardholder for replacing the gift certificate, store gift card, or general-use prepaid card or for providing the certificate or cardholder with the remaining balance in some manner before the funds expiration date unless such certificate or card has been lost or stolen. (12 CFR 205.20(e)(4))			
69. The following disclosures are provided in connection with a gift certificate, store gift card, or general-use prepaid card, as applicable:			
• For each type of fee that may be imposed in connection with the gift certificate or card (other than a dormancy, inactivity, or service fee subject to the disclosure requirements under 12 CFR 205.20(d)(2), the following information must be provided on or with the certificate or card:			
– The type of fee; (12 CFR 205.20(f)(1)(i))			
– The amount of the fee (or an explanation of how the fee will be determined); and (12 CFR 205.20(f)(1)(ii))			

EFTA Worksheet	Yes	No	NA
– The conditions under which the fee may be imposed. (12 CFR 205.20(f)(1)(iii))			
• A toll-free telephone number and, if one is maintained, a Web site, that a consumer may use to obtain information about dormancy, inactivity, service, or each type of fee that may be imposed in connection with the certificate or card. (12 CFR 205.20(f)(2))			

Laws

15 USC 1693, Electronic Fund Transfer Act
15 USC 7001 et seq., Electronic Signatures in Global and
National Commerce Act

Regulations

12 CFR 205, Electronic Fund Transfers (Regulation E)

OCC Issuances

Advisory Letter 2004–6, "Payroll Card Systems," May 6, 2004
Advisory Letter 2004–11, "Electronic Consumer Disclosures,"
October 1, 2004
OCC Bulletin 2005–9, "Overdraft Protection Programs: Interagency
Guidance," April 6, 2005
OCC Bulletin 2011–27, "Prepaid Access Programs: Risk Management
Guidance and Sound Practices," June 28, 2011